The Year of the Poet VI

of the

Poet VI

March 2019

The Poetry Posse

inner child press, ltd.

The Poetry Posse 2019

Gail Weston Shazor

Shareef Abdur Rasheed

Teresa E. Gallion

hülya n. yılmaz

Kimberly Burnham

Tzemin Ition Tsai

Elizabeth Esguerra Castillo

Jackie Davis Allen

Joe Paire

Caroline 'Ceri' Nazareno

Ashok K. Bhargava

Alicja Maria Kuberska

Swapna Behera

Albert 'Infinite' Carrasco

Eliza Segiet

William S. Peters, Sr.

General Information

The Year of the Poet VI
March 2019 Edition

The Poetry Posse

1st Edition : 2019

Publisher Information
1st Edition : Inner Child Press
intouch@innerchildpress.com
www.innerchildpress.com

$ 12.99

WHAT WOULD LIFE BE WITHOUT A LITTLE POETRY?

Dedication

This Book is dedicated to

Poetry . . .

The Poetry Posse

past, present & future

our Patrons and Readers

the Spirit of our Everlasting Muse

&

the Power of the Pen

to effectuate change!

In the darkness of my life
I heard the music
I danced . . .
and the Light appeared
and I dance

Janet P. Caldwell

Table of Contents

The Poetry Posse

Table of Contents . . . *continued*

March Featured Poets   111

Foreword

Carribbean

When i stepped into this project as a member of the Poetry Posse/Inner Child Press International and cultural ambassador i asked myself what's the most prevalent vibe you feel when you hear " The Caribbean " and immediately the first word that came to mind is diversity, immediately followed by " flavor " plenty of both. The area that constitutes the Caribbean is vast, over one million sq. miles comprised of over 700 Islands including Island nations.

In the cast bordering the Caribbean Sea, North Atlantic Ocean, South East of the Gulf of Mexico and North American mainland. East of Central America, North of South America. Personification of diversity manifest in ethnicity, language, religions, politics etc. Impacted by colonization by the likes of England, France, Spain, Portugal, Netherlands etc.

The slave trade played a major part on the region with many west Africans captured by slave traders being sent to Caribbean Islands bringing their culture, art, music, religions, etc. that had and to this day have a profound effect on the entire region. Actually the Colonial invaders that seized large swaths of territory also left their mark on the inhabitants till this day as well even though most of the Caribbean Nations have achieved independence.

Diversity also goes beyond human beings, their respective cultures, religions, etc. It spills over into Bio-diversity:

The Caribbean islands have one of the most diverse eco systems in the world. The animals, fungi and plants, and have been classified as one of Conservation International's biodiversity hotspots because of their exceptionally diverse terrestrial and marine ecosystems, ranging from montane cloud forests, to tropical rainforest, to cactus scrublands. The region also contains about 8% (by surface area) of the world's coral reefs along with extensive seagrass meadows, both of which are frequently found in the shallow marine waters bordering the island and continental coasts of the region.

Economies vary, GDP per capita (PPP) (US$) ranges as high as $32,000 (Bahamas) to $1,300 (Haiti)

Economic activity include resources for trade such as fruits, beans, wood, etc. Caribbean Islands are blessed with very fertile land for farming. Of course Tourism is the main industry that floats the economy in many of the Caribbean Island countries given beautiful tropical weather, beach's, resort facilities/hotels ideal for vacationing all year around. The region also features beautiful coral reefs and rain forests essential to the environment.

Languages include, English, Spanish, French (Creole), Dutch, etc. Culture is influenced by European, African and indigenous traditions. Two major indigenous groups are Taino in the Greater Antilles and the Caribs in the Lesser Antilles.

The Caribbean has given birth to such Notable internationally renown figures such as Haitian hero Troussant Louverture who lead the defeat of the French in Haiti lead by Napoleon in 1803. Fidel Castro (Cuba) who headed up a revolution that culminated in his being head of state. In 1959 to recently when he passed away. Along with his close comrade Che Guevara they became the standard bearers of revolution in not only Cuba but throughout the Latin American diaspora, Che Guevara especially after his execution in Bolivia became the poster boy for revolution globally. Cuba proved their resilience when the USA levied sanctions against Cuba due to their Communist leanings and relation with Russia then the USSR. Not only did they survive they thrived using a well thought out plan to maximize the resources that the Island of Cuba had and even eventually produced Physicians that they sent where needed for humanitarian aide the world over. There army spilled blood fighting against apartheid in South Africa. Students from all over who otherwise wouldn't be able to attend Medical School became MD's in Cuba. The Cuban people united and grew stronger and more resilient in adversity.

In the field of Music the Caribbean became a leading force in several genres of music. Cuba had the great Machito who with the likes of Jazz musicians like Dizzy Gillespie created the amazing Afro-Cubano Latin Jazz fusion. Joining them was the great Celia Cruz, La'lupe, Mongo Santamaria, Candido, etc. Puerto Rico had more then their share of great Salsa Ambassadors like Tito ' El Ray ' Puente, Fania All Stars, Eddie and Charlie Palmieri, Hector Lavoe, and many more. together all of them sent Latin Music around the world. In Jamaica Bob Marley and the Wailers sent Reggae around the world as a major musical genre.
In closing i haven't even began to scratch the surface of the contributions this enormous unique region of the world has made essentially through it's wonderful melting pot of many different peoples who all make the Caribbean their home.

The Poetry Posse who were formed in 2014 under the banner of Inner Child Press headed up by William S. Peter's Sr. have contributed their work collectively to address this theme: The Caribbean Enjoy the talented art form on your journey to the Caribbean. Bon Voyage.

Shareef Abdur-Rasheed
AKA Zakir Flo

Poets, Writers . . . know that we are the enchanting magicians that nourishes the seeds of dreams and thoughts . . . it is our words that entice the hearts and minds of others to believe there is something grand about the possibilities that life has to offer and our words tease it forth into action . . . for you are the Poet, the Writer to whom the Gift of Words has been entrusted . . .

~ wsp

Preface

Dear Family and Friends,

Yes I am excited? This year we have aligned our vision with that of UNESCO as it honors and acknowledges a variety of Global Indigenous cultures. We are now in our sixth year of publication. As are on our way to hitting another milestone. Needless to say, I am elated. Our initial vision was to just perform at this level for the year of 2014. Since that time we have had the blessed opportunity to include many other wonderful word artists and storytellers in the Poetry Posse from lands, cultures and persuasions all over the world. We have featured hundreds of additional poets, thereby introducing their poetic offerings to our vast global readership.

In keeping with our effort and vision to expand the awareness of poets from all walks by making this offerings accessible, we at Inner Child Press International will continue to make every volume a FREE Download. The books are also available for purchase at the affordable cost of $7.00 per volume.

In the previous years, our monthly themes were Flowers, Birds, Gemstones, Trees and Past

Cultures. This year we have elected to continue the Cultural theme. In each month's volume you will have the opportunity to not only read at least one poem themed by our Poetry Posse members about such culture, but we have included a few words about the culture in our prologue. The reasoning behind this is that now our poetry has the opportunity to be educational for not only the reader, but we poets as well. We hope you find the poetic offerings insightful as we use our poetic form to relay to you what we too have learned through our research in making our offering available to you, our readership.

In closing, we would like to thank you for being an integral part of our amazing journey.

Enjoy our amazing featured poets . . . they are amazing!

Building Cultural Bridges of Understanding . . .

Bless Up . . . From the home in our hearts to yours

Bill

The Poetry Posse
Inner Child Press Ineternational

PS

Do Not forget about the World Healing, World Peace Poetry effort.

Available here

www.worldhealingworldpeacepoetry.com

For Free Downloads of Previous Issues of The Year of the Poet

www.innerchildpress.com/the-year-of-the-poet

poetry is . . . .

The Carribean

The Caribbean cultures is a very diverse one. Over the colonization years, there have been many invasive peoples who have had a significant impact on the people and the geography. This would include the English, Dustch, Spanish to name a few. These cultures not only infused their ways, beliefs and politics upon the land, but they also disturbed the inherent ways of the indigenous peoples who inhabited these very same lands centuries before their arrival. This resulted in many atrocities visited upon these peoples as well as an exploitation and or pollution of the natural resources. Also introduced were they various African cultures as slaves, which also had a profound effect.

Poets . . .
sowing seeds in the
Conscious Garden of Life,
that those who have yet to come
may enjoy the Flowers.

I Fly

because ... said the Dreamer to the world. I Can

www.iamjustbill.com

The
Year
of the
Poet VI

March 2019

The Poetry Posse

Poetry succeeds where instruction fails.

~ wsp

Gail Weston Shazor

This is a creative promise ~ my pen will speak to and for the world. Enamored with letters and respectful of their power, I have been writing for most of my life. A mother, daughter, sister and grandmother I give what I have been given, greatfilledly.

Author of . . .

"An Overstanding of an Imperfect Love"
&
Notes from the Blue Roof

Lies My Grandfathers Told Me

available at Inner Child Press.

www.facebook.com/gailwestonshazor
www.innerchildpress.com/gail-weston-shazor
navypoet1@gmail.com

Wishing

On my wishing days
I used to wonder about wandering
I could feel the silver
Quickening in my limbs
Although I was told to lie still
On the floor
The snake oil felt cold
And I supposed it was because
Snakes are cold blooded too
I could never remember which
Indian I was in that moment
Some say it was Cherokee or
Choctaw, all I know is I needed to be still
My great grandfather walked around me
In his Indian clothes
And Indian feathers and Indian dance steps
At every pass, he smiled down at me
And I smiled back, safely stilled
Big momma whispered in my ear
From her lying place beside me
"remember this day chile,
for this is where we meet
hand to hand, heart to heart
binding you to us forever"
And I remembered the coldness
Of the snake oil on my skin
And the quickening of the silver
In my veins
Lost in the wondering of my wandering
Her hands roughened from the cotton
Never really soothed by board chalk
Snow white hands joined the negro ones

Clasped across my forehead
I could see the others swirling
Like a borned wind behind my closed eyes
I wanted to clap in delight
At the many colors, the different clothing
That they wore in celebration
Of my natural called bonekeeping
And I ever remain the wishing
In the embrace of my family

Hireath

I would that this speaks in tongues to you
Speaks in tongues that only you understand
Where the sound of my colors shine brightly
Into your everyday life
Recall my flavor
And you will miss me when you wake up

I would that my ink says to you
My ink says to you the things that I cannot
Bear to have rolling off my tongue
In flavors I may not like the taste of
So I sip at it
When I should just take a bite

And I long for my place next to you
The next to you place after a long walk in the cold
Where you can warm me
From the core
Of heat and warmth and love
That I can no longer find in this space

I try not to be sad when I think of you
When I think of you and me in our yesterdays
How can something so sweet
Hurt so much
But I know I can never turn time on itself
And my heart remains a memory

Famous Five

But there are acts and qualities necessary for intimacy to
be sustained. Strength, for instance.

(my 5:
Strength
Courage
Wisdom
Faith
Loyalty)

You loved me from the beginning
When I was just a future
Unheard and unseen
Unspoken into your existence
And yet, I knew I would come to you
You, of courage to see me
The strength it must have taken
To believe in faith
In possibilities and yet
We faltered
In that wisdom of truth
I am here and you are there
Or
I am not there and you are not here
The number of words is irreverent
When the soul has been cleaved
Much as counting grains of rice
On an empty belly
There used to be tears
So many that they created an ocean

Between us
Now they only come on days
That have a full moon
My love is loyal for your heart
The distance can be breached
By prayers

Alicja
Maria
Kuberska

.

Alicja Maria Kuberska – awarded Polish poetess, novelist, journalist, editor. She was born in 1960, in Świebodzin, Poland. She now lives in Inowrocław, Poland.
In 2011 she published her first volume of poems entitled: "The Glass Reality". Her second volume "Analysis of Feelings", was published in 2012. The third collection "Moments" was published in English in 2014, both in Poland and in the USA. In 2014, she also published the novel - "Virtual roses" and volume of poems "On the border of dream". Next year her volume entitled "Girl in the Mirror" was published in the UK and "Love me" , " (Not)my poem" in the USA. In 2015 she also edited anthology entitled "The Other Side of the Screen".

In 2016 she edited two volumes: "Taste of Love" (USA), "Thief of Dreams" (Poland) and international anthology entitled " Love is like Air" (USA). In 2017 she published volume entitled "View from the window" (Poland). She also edits series of anthologies entitled "Metaphor of Contemporary" (Poland)

Her poems have been published in numerous anthologies and magazines in Poland, the USA, the UK, Albania, Belgium, Chile, Spain, Israel, Canada, India, Italy, Uzbekistan, Czech Republic, South Korea and Australia. She was a featured poet of New Mirage Journal (USA) in the summer of 2011.

Alicja Kuberska is a member of the Polish Writers Associations in Warsaw, Poland and IWA Bogdani, Albania. She is also a member of directors' board of Soflay Literature Foundation.

Columbia

I travel to the country of a thousand colors
To see stone tears of despair of the goddess Fura.
I behold how they shine and sparkle in dark green
With a bit of blue sky and water trapped inside them.
Green specks flicker in the amazing crystals.

In a cup of coffee I find an unknown aromatherapy.
I love the taste and aroma of this black drink
Which is precious like ancient Indian gold.
It awakens the senses and tempts the newcomers.
A piece of chocolate completes my feast.

The sellers peddle many exotic fruits on their stalls.
They offer the richness and generosity of nature.
The plentitude of colors and flavors are amazing.
The motley agave baskets hang next to them.
As the legend says, they choose the owners.

The Meeting Place

Our favorite bar exists in time and space.
Nothing changes there.
The floor like a mirror reflects lights
In shades of sky- blue and navy.

Bartender,
Trustee of love's mysteries,
With the face of a Sphinx,
Concocts love potions
Or collects tears in chalices.

I heard only your voice.
I held you by the hand.
The fingers trembled eagerly.
I saw only your eyes.
We were alone in the crowd.
We found the silence among sounds.

We can return to here, where all began.
Let's write another episode of life.
Our barstools like giraffes will reach the sky.
The bartender will smile
And give us another magic elixir

After the frost

I wander alone in the autumn park
And the paths lead me increasingly towards winter.
The trees have turned their rich palette of colors
Into a mossy nudity of the twisted branches.
The air is empty without birds' chirping
And the joyful chatter of children at play.
The traces of the swan's feathers
Disappeared from the pond
And kisses of lovers hide deeply in my memory
Winds whistles on lifeless grasses
And break the dry branches with a wailing groan
Moisture spreads a glassy shroud onto the ground
And hibernation - a mirror image of death enters
I notice the melancholic charm of passing away
In the eternal cycle of the seasons
I learn from the fallen leaves,
Twisted like ancient scrolls,
And crumbling in the gray
Footsteps sound loudly in the silence
Of frozen gravel, cracking on the path
The loud croaking of the flying crow's flock
Points my thoughts in the direction of next spring.

Jackie
Davis
Allen

Jackie Davis Allen, otherwise known as Jacqueline D. Allen or Jackie Allen, grew up in the Cumberland Mountains of Appalachia. As the next eldest daughter of a coal miner father and a stay at home mother, she was the first in her family to attend and graduate from college. Her siblings, in their own right, are accomplished, though she is the only one, to date, that has discovered the gift of writing.

Graduating from Radford University, with a Bachelors of Science degree in Early Education, she taught in both public and private schools. For over a decade she taught private art classes to children both in her home and at a local Art and Framing Shop where she also sold her original soft sculptured Victorian dolls and original christening gowns.

She resides in northern Virginia with her husband, taking much needed get-aways to their mountain home near the Blue Ridge Mountains, a place that evokes memories of days spent growing up in the Appalachian Mountains.

A lover of hats, she has worn many. Following marriage to her college sweetheart, and as wife, mother, grandmother, teacher, tutor, artist, writer, poet and crafter, she is a lover of art and antiques, surrounding herself, always, with books, seeking to learn more.

In 2015 she authored *Looking for Rainbows, Poetry, Prose and Art*, and in 2017, *Dark Side of the Moon*. Both books of mostly narrative poetry were published by Inner Child Press and were edited by hulya n. yilmaz.

http://www.innerchildpress.com/jackie-davis-allen.php
jackiedavisallen.com

Jackie Davis Allen

Dreaming of the Caribbean

Sun, sea and sand. . .
A land of islands, numbering in the hundreds.
        A source of wonder, inspiration for vacations.
           A place inhabited mostly by wildlife;
             A place I visit in my dreams.
And yet there's far more. . .
The food, its culinary influenced by the world;
        Seasoned with the taste of Africa, China, Spain.
           East India. Perhaps even France?
           Just the thought of it makes me drool.

Ah...breathe in the fresh, clean pure air. . .
Taste the pineapples, pigeon peas, jerk chicken.
        See the iridescent birds, shells, orchids, palms;
        And, the hibiscus, like one in my stateside lawn.
        Drink in a sweet pineapple-rum infused drink.

Savor the musical genres. . .
Listen to, and dance to, reggae, calypso, salsa. More.
        Sway to the rhythm of the drums, the steel pans!
        Tourists often choose to return. Year after year.
           See the nearby cruise ships?

Oh, the atmosphere. . .
The Caribbean culture beckons!
        So too, her stunning beaches; perhaps
        One day, I'll step outside of my dream
        Onto the sands of one of its exotic islands.

Wings of Prayer

Dazzling bright sunlight
Greets me as morning's dawn
Fades into clouds of accumulating memory.

And awesome are the ancestral gifts
Of love and liberty;
And for the gift I am now claiming:
Trying out my wings, not simply content
To stay in the nest of restlessness.

'Tis a reign of accomplishment,
Sitting or by chance dreaming,
Collecting visions and weaving creative scenes.

Of the past, of my tomorrows
Some disappointing weavings shallsurely linger
Into the velvet night of thought.
I am sequestered into a dark nest of foreboding;
But not for long, for it is to God that I belong.

One strand plucked from here. And one
From there! The sharp and yellowed beak
Of earlier day's unwelcome tidings, strain, stress!

But the mature and fledgling offspring
Of mind's thought passionately and hungrily cries out
Attempting to loosen the tight weavings!
Wavering, I am in the overshadowing trees
Longing, venturing out to capture the slightest breeze.

Strong yet bending, comes the engulfing night
Which welcomes me long past midnight.
I sense, and recall more; am anxious, desiring to flee!

To a solitary place I drift as if by midnight's lace~
And, as moon, and stars' silvery silence sift down ,
I relinquish memory mind weavings, and venture out
In prayer, capturing moonbeam's ray of hope.
Arrayed only in barest branch-twig's overcoat.

Truth's dazzling bright sunlight
Greets me as morning's dawn arrives, night
Passes into fading clouds of memory.

And, awesome are the ancestral gifts
Woven from love and liberty.
And great is the gift I am now claiming.
I give thanks to the Almighty,
Who softly reassures, "I am with you always."

The Dream

Twisted, gnarled branches
Silhouetted against the darkening sky
Blackbirds flocking, squawking
Fleeing the sorrowful
Wind swept landscape of a child's sigh

Torrential rains
Striking, frightening, wounding
Ravens hiding
Cawing, cawing, crying
Over anticipated desire for life's symphony

Dayspring, summer flowers
Sprouting, emerging
Bluebirds chirping, singing
Returning, renewing nature
And desiring something more

Hot, bright scalding light
Stinging, burning notes
Composing, orchestrating
A song, a chorus
Of a future awakening to possibilities

Twisted, gnarled branches
Torrential rains; dayspring, summer flowers
Hot bright scalding light
Tireless efforts revealing
Childhood's dream now in sight

Tzemin
Ition
Tsai

Dr. Tzemin Ition Tsai (蔡澤民博士) was born in Tzemin Ition Tsai Taiwan, Republic of China, in 1957. He holds a Ph.D. in Chemical Engineering and two Masters of Science in Applied Mathematics and Chemical Engineering. He is an associate professor at the Asia University (Taiwan), editor of "Reading, Writing and Teaching" academic text. He also writes the long-term columns for Chinese Language Monthly in Taiwan.

He is a scholar with a wide range of expertise, while maintaining a common and positive interest in science, engineering and literature member.

He has won many national literary awards. His literary works have been anthologized and published in books, journals, and newspapers in more than 40 countries and have been translated into more than a dozen languages.

Capriccios of The Caribbean Sea

Seawater
Indiscriminately invading my beach
Dark blue dark
Light green light
My hometown far from ten thousand miles away
Why as I looked at the distant places along the Gulf of
Mexico
My mind should be blocking by the sound of waves that
were far away

My hometown
Also living a group of aborigines
Like them
In the name of the Antilles
When the sound of the drums and the wolf smoke sway in
the soul
Childhood memories
Melting my heart for my ancestral soul

How to understand
This whine
Unable to saw through the vast waters of the Pacific Ocean
I was standing at
West of the Great Antilles
One step forward
Until the ice-cold feeling drowned my chest

The Path That Full of Plum Blossoms

Did not want to stay
The late autumn still hurried away
The autumn wind must never let the maple leaves remain
When red was completely faded
Drunk guest in blue shirts were not waiting for the sky to
be full of white
There are countless plum blossoms
Little green fruit
Hiding in the leaves

Swallows flying
Green water quietly around the countryside
Can't tolerate a little bit of untidy noise
That came swarming crowd
The wind blew again
No one couldn't tell the difference between drunk and not-
drunk
Poincettia can only be disguised as
Snowy

Under the high trees
Beauties played on the swings
White clothes, white clouds, white snowflakes
Laughter continually interrupted
Didn't allow the spring not to back
Unlimited reverie
Always like to say there are other fish
In the sea

Leading My Way

The colored pointed building looks down at the ferry port
Sadness be drifted
By the curtain with hanging beads
Heartbroken rhymes
Let the horse run wild with it thousands of miles away

A banquet in the hall
Beauties move in high society
Slightly frowned eyebrows accompanied by piano sound
Colorful candle smog everywhere
Sipping a glass of wine
Waiting for that slight tipsy will come here
To poke fun at me

Colorful embroidery screen
A pair of Mandarin ducks snuggled each other
Spring fills the air with warmth
Surrounds the shadow of the cloister
The bells were sparse in the moonlight
In the midst of joy
How many fascinating sceneries
Leaving song on the pillow softly killing me

Letterhead that sealed the traces of tears
Huge palace boat
Carrying away from the sorrow of leaving hometown
With the afterglow of the setting sun
Far away and gradually disappear
Should I fold a branch of plum blossom?
Send it to the grass to lead the way
Where can I retrieve my lover?

Shareef Abdur Rasheed

Shareef Abdur-Rasheed, AKA Zakir Flo was born and raised in Brooklyn, New York. His education includes Brooklyn College, Suffolk County Community College and Makkah, Saudi Arabia. He is a Veteran of the Viet Nam era, where in 1969 he reverted to his now reverently embraced Islamic Faith. He is very active in the Islamic community and beyond with his teachings, activism and his humanity.

Shareef's spiritual expression comes through the persona of "Zakir Flo" . Zakir is Arabic for "To remind". Never silent, Shareef Abdur-Rasheed is always dropping science, love, consciousness and signs of the time in rhyme.

Shareef is the Patriarch of the Abdur-Rasheed Family with 9 Children (6 Sons and 3 Daughters) and 41 Grandchildren (24 Boys and 17 Girls).

For more information about Shareef, visit his personal FaceBook Page at :

https://www.facebook.com/shareef.abdurrasheed1
https://zakirflo.wordpress.com

Dem..,

flaming hot carob in pot
be it shrimp, beef, goat,
ox tails,
jerk chicken or not
ingredients: soul, heart,
island smart, blessed parts
grow in tropical sun
abundance from mother earth
dem fertile, crops,
mama's and pops
jump up family collective
bigups
respect-of the island's
bounties
including its inhabitants diverse
as the herbs, plants, all enhance
jubilee, celebration, song, dance
Caribbean people, human bouquet,
mosaic melody played in harmony
one love!
Robert Nesta Marley, Bunny,
Whalers, players,
Caribbean rich flavor, power
fuels spiritual, mental, physical,
desire
lights perpetual fires
because carob is,
~Hot ~ Hot ~ Hot ~
my posse jump up
respect ceee.
i want to be free, sleep on a white
sand beach under a palm tree

singing: get up, stand up for your
rights, so women don't cry
please.,
let me see Caribbean Sea on a
moon lite, star filled night
holding my main squeeze tight
you know that's right
meanwhile, blue mountains
smile looking over
Caribbean Sea

food4thought = education

preoccupied..,

life bounces one around
left, right, up, down
finally, in the ground
is the sound
called reality
and your peeps
get a preview, sneak peak
while caught up in the grief
of what awaits
there will come a time
when your name is mentioned
it will begin with ' The Late '

nothing owed, nothing owned
except your deeds
determine eternal home
for your soul
if creator's mercy intercedes
soul planted like a seed
in Firdous, Jannah, paradise

meanwhile mankind preoccupied
with temporary endeavors
like ya'll living forever
but you won't
can you take anything you so love
from the things that mean sooo much
on the journey that awaits?
absolutely not!
so, what do you actually got?
considering keeping it is not
an option

nor your wife, children, Big job
the fine crib in which you live
that ride that puffed you up with pride
now is somebody else's,
why?
cause you died
can't no one take nothing,
none of that
to the other side
so much for being
preoccupied

food4thought = education

FLIP

caught up
in the blandness of routine
brought up in the madness
of the scene
Increasingly growing insensitive
a numbing effect
like novacaine you inject
signs of the times
that seem strange
Ignored by minds
that reject change
explored not the dynamics
of this trip
to calculate the mathematics
of life's flip
today what is deemed fantastic
tomorrow flips like gymnastics
such is the reality of this
much is disguised
so, you didn't realize
the demise of what you
thought was bliss
but upon inspection
turns out to be pure deception
but since conception
the reality is our mortality
that death will visit every soul
is truth in totality
that the one who has power
over all things is what stands
between us and calamity
is real not insanity

man's attraction to fleshly satisfaction
causes a reaction
to be trippin and forget life be flippin

you're not here then you born,
your here and then you're gone
joy and sorrow, lend then borrow,
here today, gone tomorrow
dem be trippin, life be flippin
no matter what you think
life be flippin before you can blink
man plans, Allah Plans and
Allah is the best of planers
it's a reality only Allah stands
between us and calamity

food4thought = education

Kimberly Burnham

Find yourself in the pattern. As a 28-year-old photographer, Kimberly Burnham appreciated beauty. Then an ophthalmologist diagnosed her with a genetic eye condition saying, "Consider life, if you become blind." She discovered a healing path with insight, magnificence, and vision. Today, 33 years later, a poet and neurosciences expert with a PhD in Integrative Medicine, Kimberly's life mission is to change the global face of brain health. Using health coaching, Reiki, Matrix Energetics, craniosacral therapy, acupressure, and energy medicine, she supports people in their healing from brain, nervous system, and chronic pain issues. As managing editor of Inner Child Magazine, Kimberly's 2019 project is peace, language, and visionary poetry with her recently published book, *Awakenings: Peace Dictionary, Language and the Mind, a Daily Brain Health Program.*

http://www.NerveWhisperer.Solutions
https://www.linkedin.com/in/kimberlyburnham

Start Calm in the Caribbean

There is a saying in Guadeloupian Creole French
where "pé" from the French "paix" is peace or calm
"ou pé komansé dékòlè"
—you can start calm
or you can calm down now—
and I imagine the situations
where I start calm at the beach
with a gentle ocean breeze
or diving amongst colorful fish
and times when I have to calm down
when small things go wrong
and I forget for a moment how truly lucky I am
to be able to vacation in the sun of Guadeloupe

Many Languages Travel in Shanti

"Shánti" or "Sjaantie"
peace in Caribbean Hindustani
which of course sounds misplaced
as if Hindustani with 29 million native speakers
and "shanti" should all live in peace
a world away in India

Caribbean Hindustani "lingua franca"
fueled by the Indo-Caribbean diaspora
words based on Bhojpuri with influences from Awadhi

"Shānti" "sakoon" or "aman"
peace in Bhojpuri spoken in Uttar Pradesh of North India
Mauritius and the Madhesh of Nepal

"Aman" peace in today's Awadhi
spoken in India and Nepal

Languages of indentured laborers
immigrants to the Caribbean from the Indian subcontinent
related to Fiji Hindi, the Bhojpuri spoken in Mauritius
and the Hindustani spoken in South Africa

All the words traveling in peace
from one place to another

Vrede: All the Peace Between Asking and The Unusual

"Vrede" is peace in Dutch
lurking in the dictionary near the foreign and the unusual
"vragen" to ask, to charge, to require
"vrede" peace required
hoping there is no need for "vredesmacht" peacekeeping
forces
"in vredesnaam" for goodness sake
just find a "vredestichter" peacemaker
deal "vredig" peacefully and be "vreedzaam" peaceable
in encounters that are "vreemd"
strange, foreign, alien
in lands "vreemde" abroad
and among people "vreemdeling" strangers, foreigners
found today in the "vreemdelingenverkeer" tourist traffic
and "vreemd'soortig" all things and people unusual
to be discovered in the Netherlands
Belgium, Suriname, the Caribbean
Indonesia, South Africa and beyond

Elizabeth E. Castillo

Elizabeth Esguerra Castillo is a multi-awarded and an Internationally-Published Contemporary Author/Poet and a Professional Writer / Creative Writer / Feature Writer / Journalist / Travel Writer from the Philippines. She has 2 published books, "Seasons of Emotions" (UK) and "Inner Reflections of the Muse", (USA). Elizabeth is also a co-author to more than 60 international anthologies in the USA, Canada, UK, Romania, India. She is a Contributing Editor of Inner Child Magazine, USA and an Advisory Board Member of Reflection Magazine, an international literary magazine. She is a member of the American Authors Association (AAA) and PEN International.

Web links:

Facebook Fan Page

https://free.facebook.com/ElizabethEsguerraCastillo

Google Plus

https://plus.google.com/u/0/+ElizabethCastillo

The Arawaks

God gave these people such wonderful gifts-
Endowed with natural resources,
They created elaborate pottery, such a talented tribe
A complex culture they have thrived.

Arawaks are known to believe in nature spirits and
ancestors,
Likened to the hierarchies of chiefs, this depicts their
religion
By the foothills of the mystic Andes they roam,
Though remained isolated from Andean civilization.

Like any other indigenous people,
The Arawaks gave the world such amazing contributions
From the time Christopher Columbus discovered them in
Hispaniola,
The first native people he has ever encountered in his
expeditions.

One Fine Day

Those eyes will look at me-

Bewildered, not

You will realize-

It has always been me-

One fine day-

Our gaze will meet-

To capture this moment in time.

Lighthouse

I thought death was at my door-
Been knockin' in my head,
I thought it was the end-
But then you approached me
You light up my darkest nights-
When I used to succumb to an abyss of incertainty-
You became the Lighthouse and rescued me.

Joe
Paire

Joseph L Paire' aka Joe DaVerbal Minddancer . . .
is a quiet man, born in a time where civil liberties
were a walk on thin ice. He's been a victim of his
own shyness often sidelined in his own quest for
love. He became the observer, charting life's path.
Taking note of the why, people do what they do.
His writings oft times strike a cord with the
dormant strings of the reader. His pen the rosined
bow drawn across the mind. He comes full-frontal
or in the subtlest way, always expressing in a way
that stimulate the senses.

www.facebook.com/joe.minddancer

Island Dreams

In the sun with coconuts
Mixed fruit drink fills my cup
I'm in the Caribbean
My dreams I'm living them
I've seen the living Sun
It beams and tans
It bleaches the sand
A comfort of man
That pales in northern light
Spicy delights delectable bites
The people there, dwell in harmony
The flavor there has this hold on me
Island dreams and I awake to ice and snow
My back hurts from shoveling you know?
Call it culture shock or just a want; to go
A week or two is not enough
Just ask anyone not there
driving the evening rush
So many places to visit and sample
So much richness in its music example
Steel drums Steel Pulse still leaving the coast
Still fishing in waters that rule its host
We the visitors who doing the most
Let us not forget the native life
It's more than flora or fauna or breezes in the night
The Caribbean breathes through lungs unseen
I live my island dreams

Ashes To Ashes

I gazed upon a beautiful urn today
Dotted pews with weepers
Hugs from long time no see are kin to me
Failing memories keep the names at bey
But to a few, I can still hey how you been
There's a thin border between family and friend
I must ask who's who before I commit a sin
A church hug in a church and I'm back to remember when
Black suits and ties, hoodies and jeans
Children running around unaware of the scene
That's the beauty of life as untainted minds scheme
Who'll remember you after your transition
Who'll prepare the meals and bless the food
What family matriarch will oversee the crew
Death is a beautiful thing as tragic as it is
We we're born to die
Who teaches you to live?
Ashes to ashes as we struggle to survive
Stretching the inevitable unable to give
No longer cared for just cared for in past tense
Left to wonder in thought what's beyond the fence
A meet and greet on the other side
No pain no worries and a thousand brides
Right now, there's fear of the unknown
No one wants to go and go we must
Ashes to ashes and dust to dust

Climate Change

There's a cold front approaching
Where can I go?
Some folk runaway from ice and snow

Some folk loath the heat of summer
They travel to places to cold to wander in
So I'm wondering why the change?

Have you ever been climatized?
It's been zero degrees for two weeks
Now it's 30 degrees and you feel the heat

I've seen it 40 degrees
people start wearing shorts
believe you me

The temperature is 72 degrees
People are wearing jackets and coats
But they're from Hawaii you see?

A scalding hot tub feels good in a few minutes
That inrush of breath when you stick your toe in it
Then soak and hope and dream, savoring the steam

Climate change is truly a global thing
It's getting warmer and warmer
The scientist has warned you, informed you

But I digress back to the degrees
32, is freezing water, Arizona got dry heat
Hazy, hot and humid does it for me

hülya
n.
yılmaz

A retired Liberal Arts professor, hülya n. yılmaz [sic] is Co-Chair and Director of Editing Services at Inner Child Press International, and a literary translator. Her poetry has been published in an excess of sixty anthologies of global endeavors. Two of her poems are permanently installed in *TelePoem Booth*, a nation-wide public art exhibition in the U.S. She has shared her work in Kosovo, Canada, Jordan and Tunisia. hülya has been honored with a 2018 WIN Award of British Colombia, Canada. She is presently working on three poetry books and a short-story collection. hülya finds it vital for everyone to understand a deeper sense of self and writes creatively to attain a comprehensive awareness for and development of our humanity.

hülya n. yılmaz, Ph.D.

Writing Web Site
hulyanyilmaz.com

Editing Web Site
hulyasfreelancing.com

hülya n. yılmaz

The Europeans Came

Again
And did their own thing
Again

What is their own thing, you wonder?
It is quite simple, you see: to discover
What had already been duly discovered
And nurtured long before their time,
To plunder and plagiarize history,
To force assimilation and kill,
If such acts of kindness
Upon the inhabitants
Of the "new" land
Were not met
With a "Welcome!" mat.

Who lived in the Caribbean
Before the savages arrived there?

Don't rely on my words.
Check the books of his-tory.

Oh, wait!
I forgot all about that refined, timeless craft
Of the Europeans, made for their own clueless kind
And their fairy-tale-loving, unaware *off springs*,
Their nefariously steady, eras-surpassing move
To historically "re-construct" all facts anew,
Which is also known by the conscious few
As that world-renowned command:
"Under all circumstances, distract!"

Never mind then!

Just remember one fact:
There are two sides to the same coin
Which we are all tied to and frivolously spend.
One of those directions will lead you to the way
Of learning so that you are able to digest the breaking news
On the indigenous. You must be willing to listen, of course!
If or when you do, you will no longer look at that coin
In the same way ever again, for the key to awareness
Lies in between the lines . . .
Go ahead, take your pick: history by and for the Europeans,
Or the soul-narratives from the original occupants
Of the plundered land?

hülya n. yılmaz

Before the Europeans Came

"Christopher Columbus landed in the Bahamas",
Says a source.

Hmm . . . So, he did not name an unknown land himself.

I am confused.

Would you please tell me again
What exactly happened in the year of 1492?
While you are at it, do me a favor and explain to me
What is being celebrated widely
For endless times ever since?
Where have those islands' inhabitants
From mainland America, from the South,
The North, the West and the East gone then?
Yes, I mean the Ciboney, the Arawak and the Carib.

. . .

Colonization, you say?
Oh no, not that treacherous word again!
Why did you have to ruin everything for me?

And just when I was having a snack
With a cup of Columbian coffee . . .

Bartolomé de Las Casas

A Spanish cleric named as above
Gifted the conscious with a book in 1560,
History of the Indies. With it, he settles the score
Evidence-fully with the savages from Europe. In it,
He shows how the island peoples were abused and killed,
And how Europeans plagued them
With many a deadliest affliction
They had dragged along from
Their old disease-ridden,
Supposedly civil lands.

Blood-curdling is his account of
The gruesome fate of hundreds
Of villagers escaping slavery
In Trinidad: burned alive by
The Spanish leader Bono.

Why?
Because, unlike the Arawak,
The Caribs stood against their invaders.
They just would not abide . . .

Yet, the European barbarism
Had the nerve to re-write
World history:
Life came to the Caribbeans
With Christopher Columbus'
Discovery of the islands of
Cuba, Hispaniola,
Puerto Rico, etc.

Not so! But . . .
What's the difference?

The re-construction of historical facts lives on today.
Europeans would not have it any other way.
Our school books are living the evidence.

Teresa E. Gallion

Teresa E. Gallion

Teresa E. Gallion was born in Shreveport, Louisiana and moved to Illinois at the age of 15. She completed her undergraduate training at the University of Illinois Chicago and received her master's degree in Psychology from Bowling Green State University in Ohio. She retired from New Mexico state government in 2012.

She moved to New Mexico in 1987. While writing sporadically for many years, in 1998 she started reading her work in the local Albuquerque poetry community. She has been a featured reader at local coffee houses, bookstores, art galleries, museums, libraries, Outpost Performance Space, the Route 66 Festival in 2001 and the State of Oklahoma's Poetry Festival in Cheyenne, Oklahoma in 2004. She occasionally hosts an open mic.

Teresa's work is published in numerous Journals and anthologies. She has two CDs: *On the Wings of the Wind* and *Poems from Chasing Light.* She has published three books: *Walking Sacred Ground, Contemplation in the High Desert* and *Chasing Light.*

Chasing Light was a finalist in the 2013 New Mexico/Arizona Book Awards.

The surreal high desert landscape and her personal spiritual journey influence the writing of this Albuquerque poet. When she is not writing, she is committed to hiking the enchanted landscapes of New Mexico. You may preview her work at

http://bit.ly/1aIVPNq or *http://bit.ly/13IMLGh*

Caribbean Demise

Deforestation rears its ugly head
in the Caribbean Islands.

Many of the ecosystems are devastated
by deforestation, pollution and human invasion.
Animals, fungi and plants are threatened.

Increased carbon dioxide emissions and
soil erosion contributes to global warming.

Coral reefs decline at a rapid pace
as humans continue to use the seas
and oceans as garbage dumps.

Man's greed is the ultimate genocidal gun.
Freeze, do not move, death is upon you.

Leap of Faith

I leap from the cliffside
prayers tied to my feet.
Insurance for a safe landing
in the canyon bottom.

Rocks spiked by sand
form a circle around
the target I pursue.
Only faith will lead me home.

A blast through the wind
at break neck speed.
The rise and fall of pain
sheds on the down drift.

Logic says death on touchdown.
Faith makes a serene jump into life.
A soft landing gently moves the sand.

Ready to rock the earth
with my presence.
A storm trooper has landed.

No Limits

The sky is not the limit.
It is the destination,
the tease of what lies beyond,

focal point for the curious eye,
invitation to the next breath.
You may wander for days,
laid back, unconcerned.

One day a single star
may draw you
to the story yet to be told.

Ashok K. Bhargava

Ashok Bhargava is a poet, writer, community activist, public speaker, management consultant and a keen photographer. Based in Vancouver, he has published several collections of his poems: Riding the Tide, Mirror of Dreams, A Kernel of Truth, Skipping Stones, Half Open Door and Lost in the Morning Calm. His poetry has been published in various literary magazines and anthologies.

Ashok is a Poet Laureate and poet ambassador to Japan, Korea and India. He is founder of WIN: Writers International Network Canada. Its main objective is to inspire, encourage, promote and recognize writers of diverse genres, artists and community leaders. He has received many accolades including Nehru Humanitarian Award for his leadership of Writers International Network Canada, Poets without Borders Peace Award for his journeys across the globe to celebrate peace and to create alliances with poets, and Kalidasa Award for creative writings.

Caribbean Moon

follow me
to the path of the moon
to victory
we know the American
history didn't begin with Guamikena*

follow me
to the path of the moon
to silence
where stars shine
between the branches of the trees

follow me
to the path of the moon
to harmony
hear it hum
listen to it

follow me
to the path of the moon
to the edge of time
stand tall
native Indians of America

* *Guamikena is Taino Indian name for Columbus who discovered America in 1492.*
Taino Indians is a subgroup of the Arawakan Indians who inhabited Cuba, Jamaica, Haiti, the Dominican Republic, West Indies and Puerto Rico in the Caribbean Sea at the time when Christopher arrived to the New World.

What We Ask

prayer flags
tied together
hang downwards
whisper
in colorful tongues
without you ever
knowing
what we ask.

they have won. *
don't feel sorry for us.
always remember.
we are not buried.
we haven't bent
under the strength of time.
like gold
inside the mine

we will remain
pure and unmelt.
we will get
what is ours
someday.

* *Christopher Columbus was an Italian explorer who found something he wasn't looking for. In 1492 he sailed across the Atlantic Ocean, hoping to find a route to India (in order to trade for spices). He made a total of four trips to the Caribbean and South America during the years 1492-1504. Consequently, Caribbean people were colonized and their islands were looted.*

Tortuga

receding tide
leaves behind
urchins and shells.

strong winds
chisel hillside bluffs
hollowed by water.

piles of bones
tell stories
when pirates ruled the seas.

boisterous voyages
and golden booty
all that has vanished.

seashells
warm breeze and
green paradise remains.

Tortuga Island is a Caribbean island that forms part of Haiti, off the northwest coast of Hispaniola. In the 17th century, Tortuga was a major center and haven of Caribbean piracy.

Caroline
'Ceri Naz'
Nazareno

Carolin 'Ceri' Nazareno

Caroline Nazareno-Gabis a.k.a. Ceri Naz, born in Anda, Pangasinan known as a 'poet of peace and friendship', is a multi-awarded poet, journalist, editor, publicist, linguist, educator, and women's advocate.

Graduated cum laude with the degree of Bachelor of Elementary Education, specialized in General Science at Pangasinan State University. Ceri have been a voracious researcher in various arts, science and literature. She volunteered in Richmond Multicultural Concerns Society, TELUS World Science, Vancouver Art Gallery, and Vancouver Aquarium.

She was privileged to be chosen as one of the Directors of Writers Capital International Foundation (WCIF), Member of the Poetry Posse, one of the Board of Directors of Galaktika ATUNIS Magazine based in Albania; the World Poetry Canada and International Director to Philippines; Global Citizen's Initiatives Member, Association for Women's rights in Development (AWID) and Anacbanua. She has been a 4th Placer in World Union of Poets Poetry Prize 2016, Writers International Network-Canada ''Amazing Poet 2015'', The Frang Bardhi Literary Prize 2014 (Albania), the sair-gazeteci or Poet-Journalist Award 2014 (Tuzla, Istanbul, Turkey) and World Poetry Empowered Poet 2013 (Vancouver, Canada).

Caribbean Dream

Augustine's best moment
the month of engagement
found no excuses
 an extravagant excitement
the proposal was a winning game
four days before the day of hearts
Saturn rings, emblem of lust
runaway bride and groom
feet on cobblestones,
ready for the Caribbean cruise,
just checking out,
alarm clock's said,
stop dreaming!

Take Me Far

Where my feet fits the sand
Where my body feels the sun's embrace
Where my spirit lives in horizon
Where you and I spend more sunsets
Wherever, making life in our years.

Dalhin Mo Ako Sa Malayo
(Filipino)

Kung saan, nakayapak sa kabuhanginan
Kung saan, ang araw'y ako ang yakap
Kung saan, kaluluwa'y nasa alapaap
Kung saan, saksi tayo ng mga dapithapon
Saanman, may buhay sa lahat ng oras.

silhouette

i waited for the songs
of symphonic silhouette,
rhymed in accordion
of wave-like-mnemonics,
while traversing the sand
the sea and the sun,
our feet couldn't
measure the happiness
set in miles and miles deep,
like zillion ways to fly.

Swapna Behera

Swapna Behera is a bilingual contemporary poet, author, translator and editor from Odisha, India .She was a teacher from 1984 to 2015 . Her stories, poems and articles are widely published in National and International journals, and ezines, and are translated into different national and International languages. She has penned four books. She was conferred upon the Prestigious International Poesis Award of Honor at the 2nd Bharat Award for Literature as Jury in 2015, The Enchanting Muse Award in India World Poetree Festival 2017, World Icon of Peace Award in 2017, and the Pentasi B World Fellow Poet in 2017.. She is the recipient of Gold Cross Of Wisdom Award ,the medal for The Best Teachers of the World from World Union of Poets in 2018, and The LIfe time Achievement Award ,The Best Planner Award, The Sahitya Shiromani Award, ATAL BiHARI BAJPAYEE AWARD 2018, Ambassador De Literature Award 2018 .She is the Ambassador of Humanity by Hafrikan Prince Art World Africa 2018 and an official member of World Nation's Writers Union ,Kazakhstan2018. At present she is the manager at Large, Planner and Columnist of The Literati, the administrator of several poetic groups ,the member of the Special Council of Five of World Union of Poets and the Cultural Ambassador of Inner Child Press U.S.

Pour Some Sugar on Me

Pour some sugar on me
Ahh! my sentient dreams
I, the indentured labourer
Migrated from my root
A traveller having the blue sky
But no soil of my own
No flags to bear
Carried away at the age of twelve

Pour some sugar on me
Let me be sweet enough
Here I work all day
Damn tired ;
I repeat, I like my soil
Wish to melt in the dust of my village

Pour some sugar on me
Let me be as white as your tea cup
The burning sensation of my palm
The pain of Caribbean Diaspora
I lost my valley
My Paradise land, the myths
cassava porridge, songs
silk cotton trees
 rivers and tall mountains
The salt of my blood changed into sugar
My teardrops converted to concrete flood
I will be born again
From your crematorium
Fly high to weave my web
Like a spider

Pour some sugar on me
Let me be the sweetest sugar candy of this planet
Pray for my chunk of sky
That looks like your so called sugar!!!

Meditation on the Local Train

Is meditation a prank of
Inhale and exhale?
In the crowd or
 sitting alone near
the window seat
of a local train?
A man in silent mode tries
his existence beyond his I Card, Debit Cards
A woman with curly hair
struggling to fix the pillow for obesity
Her husband smiles mischievously
Exchange of love via main road
and bypass heart angiograms

The solitary man conciliates
To be romantic reaching home at night
The vendors foaming tea and coffee
In the weekend train
The rumbling tracks, sound of A.C
puffed rice with onion smell

the man meditates
dreams to love and kiss
Yes, he is in illusion
His wife's radiant smiles, seductive curves
Son's cycle race
He is fixing his concentration
To be good, better and the best
But time is dew drops on the grass
So many assignments and so less time
The local train rumbles, creeps
The man dozes

His head nods
Saliva drips from the corner of lips
Perhaps dreaming is
The climax of all meditations!!

How Does It Matter

Hello, hello who is on the line?
Oh!! You begged apology
For what?
It is too late now
Your last puffs of cigarettes still on the floor
But how does it matter
I am pregnant
Carrying you ......
Another you ....
So how does it matter !!!......

Albert 'Infinite' Carrasco

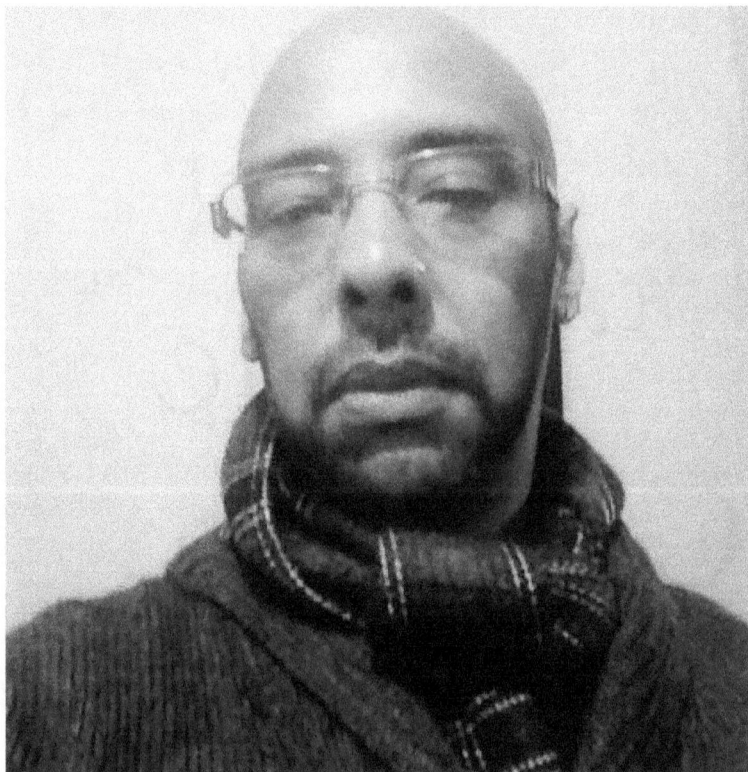

I'm a project life philanthropist, I speak about the non ethical treatment of poor ghetto people. Why? My family was their equal, my great grandmother and great grandfather was poor, my grandmother and grandfather, my mother and father, poverty to my family was a sequel, a traditional Inheritance of the subliminal. I paid attention to the decades of regression, i tried to make change, but when I came to the fork in the road and looked at the signs that read wrong < > right, I chose the left, the wrong direction, because of street life interactions a lot around me met death or incarceration. I failed myself and others. I regret my decisions, I can't reincarnate dead men, but I can give written visions in laymens. I'm back at that fork in the road, instead of it saying wrong or right, I changed it, now it says dead men < > life.

Infinite poetry @lulu.com

Alcarrasco2 on YouTube

Infinite the poet on reverbnation

Infinite Poetry

http://www.lulu.com/us/en/shop/al-infinite-carrasco/infinite-poetry/paperback/product-21040240.html

South America

Our roots trace back to South America,
Mapuche,
Quechua
And Inca.
We're from,
Ecuador,
Central Andes,
Peru,
Bolivia,
Chile an Argentina.
Although Christianity is our main religion,
Some are Jews and Muslims
There's also Judaism,
Buddhist,
Bahá'í faith and Hinduism.
Our traditional food varies in different areas like,
Empanadas, steak and chimichurri in Argentina
Cuy and aji Amarillo in Peru,
Feijoda in Brazil and Arepas in Venezuela and Columbia.
The Pacific Ocean and the Atlantic Ocean
Are our bordering bodies of water.

Before they start

I have to get to them before they start because if they do it's highly likely that they're going to be lost forever, endings aren't pretty, it's usually football numbers or murder, only a very few got the opportunity to turn dirty money into clean paper. The numbers are so minute I try not to advertise that while talking bout fast loot. To some that's logic, to others it's like cosigning the thoughts of living entire lives off drug profit. The game never changes, only the players do, I understand why these youngens are on the block... poverty.... the same reason why me and thousands of hustlers was out there too. Back then none of us had direction, luckily they have me to explain what we went through with urban poetic narrations. It became my form of expression while dealing with harsh learnt lessons. I guess I had to live it in order to teach it so every time I tap keys, push a pen or grab a mic class is in session. My life was a movie...love, action and drama, my writings paint a perfect picture but those visions will be clearer when I reach tribeca. History of the streets can help the present choose not to let history repeat, so I tell all from counting mass amount of money, to gourmet meals chased by bubbly, to homies bodies on the streets covered with bloody white sheets

Roll up

I knew they was gonna roll up on sight... Inf where's the gun? I don't have one, watcha doing out here? I'm living life, well you're on a drug block that's well known, to you it's a trap, to me it's called home. We know who you are and what you do, yeah I'm a product from an environment you're not used to.

They tried to catch me with the burner or work daily, they'll stop the whip, illegally search, they're not even ask'n for id. The streets was my way out of poverty, they knew that, so they keep jumping out try'n to get lucky. The same went for the entire team too, we were all hungry and worked as a unit as we tried to make the American dream come true.

Lines gathered from daylight to midnight, pockets got tight, sneaker box banks look'n right, went from derringers and hoopties to nines with beams and lined up Europeans. We was hot but no matter what we was gonna reach the top whether it was table grind'n or Pyrex pot.

Everyone is shinning look'n like a millie, we blew, i wish their blood stayed blue but I saw red leak from my cru, our obsession with ending depression ended for most by assassination, gettn money was easy, stay'n alive was the hard part, I remember the start as well as when those around me at that time had to depart due to no brainwaves and pulsating hearts.

Eliza Segiet

After earning a Master's Degree in Philosophy at the Jagiellonian University in Krakaw, Poland, Eliza Segiet proceeded with her post-graduate studies in the fields of Cultural Knowledge, Penal Revenue and Economic Criminal Law, Arts and Literature and Film and Television Production in the Polish city, Lodz.

With specific regard to her creative writings, the author describes herself as being torn in her passion for engaging in two literary genres: Poetry and Drama. A similar dichotomy from within is reflected on Segiet's own words about her true nature: She likes to look at the clouds, but she keeps both of her feet set firmly on the ground.

The author describes her worldview as being in harmony with that of Arthur Schopenhauer: "Ordinary people merely think how they shall 'spend' their time; a man of talent tries to 'use' it".

Be Yourself

Between the lands,
life occurs,
under the crystal panel –
another world.

A multi-colored,
delightful agitation
that one can become part of.

For a few moments
breathing differently,
looking closer,
experiencing anew.

In the vastness of the depths
underwater magic takes place.

Even for a moment,
forgetting that our place is above,

where breathing in and out
do not require thinking.
Where the needs
are getting bigger.

Becoming a fish,
compelling admiration,
not exceeding one's own abilities.

Just:

Be.

Be – yourself.

Turquoise

Our eyes
need sight.

Body – feelings.

Mind –
a treat from everyday life.

Work – home, home – work.

Someday one must say:

enough.

Where has joy hidden?
Between the sense and nonsense of life?

A long lost paradise
needs to be revealed.

So far and at the same time so close,
time can be measured
with the high and low tides
of turquoise.

To live, live
to at least

restore the meaning.

Yesterday Is in Me

Yesterday is in me,
yesterday is still going on.
Tomorrow is just about to be.
Will tomorrow stay?
A trace of what was-
the memory of the theater of life.
Still frames.
Comedy, drama, horror,
movie about love.

What will stay in me?
Joy, sadness, despair, pain, love…
Perhaps my I –
are only metaphysical possibilities?
Permeation of good and evil.

William S. Peters Sr.

Bill's writing career spans a period of over 50 years. Being first Published in 1972, Bill has since went on to Author in excess of 40 additional Volumes of Poetry, Short Stories, etc., expressing his thoughts on matters of the Heart, Spirit, Consciousness and Humanity. His primary focus is that of Love, Peace and Understanding!

Bill says . . .

I have always likened Life to that of a Garden. So, for me, Life is simply about the Seeds we Sow and Nourish. All things we "Think and Do", will "Be" Cause and eventually manifest itself to being an "Effect" within our own personal "Existences" and "Experiences" . . . whether it be Fruit, Flowers, Weeds or Barren Landscapes! Bill highly regards the Fruits of his Labor and wishes that everyone would thus go on to plant "Lovely" Seeds on "Good Ground" in their own Gardens of Life!

to connect with Bill, he is all things Inner Child

www.iaminnerchild.com

Personal Web Site

www.iamjustbill.com

Negril

on the north side of the island
walking towards West End
the Ocean's on my right side
there is nothing to defend

the waves languidly lapping
caressing my Here my Now
for Ego has surrendered
with reverence some way, some how

the Sun with love embraces
the divineness of all "BE"ing
the soft gentle breeze dusts off my lenses
and now my Soul is seeing

that all is One and One IS All
as my toes dig in the sand
i have escaped the confines of Self
and now i understand

if i but just let go and be
the limits do not exist
"i am" the genesis of what "i am"
be it anguish be it bliss

in . . .Negril . . .

Yes, I Dream
"Dedicated to all of the mis-diagnosed children of our world"

Dreams filled my head
Tumbling and running around
Looking for,
seeking
A crack in my consciousness
So that they may escape
Into the realm
Of reality

I did not mind them at all,
But sometimes they
We quite the distraction
That gave cause for me to
Forget the tasks at hand

Some people may call this
An 'Attention Deficit Disorder',
But for me
It is a realm of being
That brings me more joy
Than this world of things
I was stationed in

You wanted to give me medicine
That i may sleep,
A dreamless sleep,
But there is naught whatsoever wrong
With where I choose to be

The mundane,
The rote filled,

The rites of life
And the demand for acquiescence
And conformity
Is quite the challenge,
Whose purpose appears
To keep me from
The 'Beautiful'

In my dreams,
I can conjure,
Or create
Astounding
And magnificent
Scenarios,
And dimensions
That perhaps you
No longer understand
Since you have grown up,
But my only prayer is
That I will forever be filled
With a wonder
That transcends this reality

Won't you dream with me
Of a better tomorrow . . .
A better TODAY ?

I protest

In a flash
It was all gone . . .
Sweet memories
Of a time that used to be;
Dreams of the morrow,
Replaced with a consuming fear
And a scrambling
For survival

We had sat around
Cloaked in our indifference
As we witnessed the escalation
Of hate, greed and power
Being used as manipulative divisive devices
To serve the few

The people, yes, the people,
We the people,
Had become comfortable
With too many . . .
'Status Quos' . . .
Lorde knows
We had more power
Within us
Than we demonstrated,
Enacted,
Or exemplified

We could have changed things,
Or altered the course of events,
But most of the world's ills
Did not affect us directly,
Or profoundly,

So we wrote our little poems
Of dissent and protest,
Sang our little songs,
Went shopping,
Ate our selves
Into an oblivious consciousness
To keep from taking
The responsibility
To face a truth,
A truth about our very existence,
And do something
About it

Sure, we had words,
We signed petitions
That fell on the deaf ears
Of our rulers
Who did not give a flying "F"
Because they were being fed . . . . WELL

I for one, Protest! . . .
Who I am, who I have become
All due to my own silence,
Lethargy,
Delusional peace
And content?

Yes, I protest now,
For the way things are going,
I may not have this opportunity
Again!

March

2019

Features

Enesa Mahmić

Sylwia K. Malinowska

Shurouk Hammoud

Anwer Ghani

i Fly

because I Can

...said the Dreamer to the world.

Enesa Mahmić

Enesa Mahmić (1989) is a travel writer, an member of PEN Center.

She published 4 poetry collections. Her poems have been translated into German, Spanish, Franch, Italian, Turkish, Slovenian, Albanian and Hungarian- included in several anthologies: *Social Justice and Intersectional Feminism, University of Victoria* (Canada), I am strenght (USA) , We refugee (Australia) IFLAC antiwar and peace anthology (Israel), *Global voices of 21th century female Poets* (India), *Writing Politics and Knowledge Production* (Zimbabwe), *Spread poetry, not fear (Slovenia)*, *Le Voci della poesia* (Italy), *World for peace, World Institute for Peace* (Nigeria), and more.

She won international awards for literature: Gold medal *Neigbour of your shore 2017* as best immigrant poetry, *Ratković's Evenings of Poetry 2016* and *Aladin Lukač Award 2016* for best debut book.

Home

When I was leaving the morning was foggy.
Faces pale from insomnia
wandering toward offices, schools, banks.
Cats wailed on the roofs
Hunched old man was collecting leaves.
Nothing could have moved that eternal order
Neither could awaken lulled mass
And I went like that is possible.
I walked for a long time:
Masks and traps
And sore feet.
Soil accustomed to clatter invaders
Does not tolerate soft step.
Ghosts of the past choked me by the tough hands.
Trust me
There were all kinds of beings.
who naively were grinding too much
Ironically expressing themselves because they can not be
accepted.
There were a fleeting, perverse, idiots
Most of them were lonely.
It should be adapted to make a deal, bend the spine, lose
form.
The voice on the radio repeated:
Folks. Common will. Person. Force.
The words fell like dead birds.

I went so far
Under this sky
While my being did not cry: Home!

The Man Who Talks to Birds

Once in Forest Park
I meet a foreigner who is feeding the birds.
Last sunset of the dying autumn
Mirrored in his eyes.
He told me:
Dear friend,
My English is almost incomprehensible
I can't talk to people
I'm just sitting on banch and speaking with birds.

Enesa Mahmić

Sunday Lunch in Exile

We didn't talk about our suffering
We taught our children patience
Mastering the silent endurance
Our masters said:
Unnecessary sorrows hijack the glory of God
So, we ate the crumbs from their table
Without any complain.
We comforted ourself: *I'm fine. It's ok.*
Tomorow will be same,
The concept of discrimination repeats itself.
Gentlman from social institution will remind me again
That I'm just a number in the system.
I will be thinking again
How I should leave everything.
Maybe move to another city, another country.
I comforted myself with the illusion of love,
Understanding and forgetfulness
But deep in my heart I knew
There is no country for immigrants.

- - -

Sylwia
K.
Malinowska

Sylwia K. Malinowska is a graduate of the faculty of Journalism and Education at the University of Warsaw. A lover of Sylvia Plath and Emily Dickinson's poetry, passionate and tireless in familiarizing oneself with literature and striving at becoming an expert in it. Her poems were printed in journals such as "Poezja Dzisiaj", as well as in numerous anthologies in Polish, English and Bulgarian. She also writes poetry for the photo album by Beata Cierzniewska "Cognition" presented at The Cooper House Gallery in Dublin. The author of the literary broadcast "Black Drawer" in Dublin. She also collaborates with HelloIrlandia , which promotes Polish literature abroad. A graduate of the faculty of Journalism and Education at the University of Warsaw. A lover of Sylvia Plath and Emily Dickinson's poetry, passionate and tireless in familiarizing oneself with literature and striving at becoming an expert in it. Her poems were printed in journals such as "Poezja Dzisiaj", as well as in numerous anthologies in Polish, English and Bulgarian. She also writes poetry for the photo album by Beata Cierzniewska "Cognition" presented at The Cooper House Gallery in Dublin. The author of the literary broadcast "Black Drawer" in Dublin. She also collaborates with HelloIrlandia , which promotes Polish literature abroad.

Sylwia K. Malinowska

1.

In the Centesimal tree
In the drift of a bird
In the breasts
Devoid of milk
A divine baby with a child's head
Bare
A genuine illusion
Without a son
Without a father
Catching onto itself
His head
Her body
Adultery
Between each other
In the swaying umbilical cord
A miracle
was in less than a few moments
Leaning back
Locked in herself like a shell
A miracle
Heard the same cry
For the tenth time
Her hands
Her thighs
It must have cried out
The view was solidifying
Nobody is crying
If he was her
A peak of prosperity
And nothingness
Embryo

Stuck in development
In a totalitarian state
They sleep under water
With an open glass door
Flowers growing out of asphalt

2.

Thousands of small worlds
Hands reaching out
They stand and watch
Everything is in everything
This something tempts with charm
Recompensing for oblivion
On current existences
He will talk about her part
Like harp strings
They will not let them grow
Bigger and more numerous
Dancing on their verses
of the Culture of the age of thought
The flow of all things
The tongue touches the ear
The child itself
It remembered the door
Open to the departing
Slowly one after another
It sat on the opposite side
A line from the table
A line on the wall
In the incubators under the eyelids
Her body did not tolerate moisture
In a cramped room
The curio of here and now
The silence deserves some word
In white aprons
Inside the white
Mystery
of Eucharistic heirloom
She did not know her own height

The braver stride blindly
Desires and teases with refusal
It stayed irrevocably
Behind her back

3.

Her earthly home
A shroud with metal edges
Glass and tongue
I do not remember the body that reeks of reed
He is not the one guilty
It's a trap craving for a shout
Open the roof
They will not have anywhere to hide
In the hymn of his clamped breasts
He recalled the ones on his mind
How to heal this
Not me because I was there
My root touched him
His pieces
I discard his openness
My relative
Priceless and quiet
The ruler and the handmaid
Without missing anything
Shedding their nakedness like a scent
Like disability
Your words open up purely
They were given a black gloss
They glister
Unleashing their idol Besides me
He wanted to be good
He floats in the ganglions of her head
She seems to speak

Shurouk Hammoud

Shurouk Hammoud: a Syrian poetess, journalist and literary translator. She has five published poetry collections.

Winner of many poetry awards:

Charles Baudelaire first prize for poetry creativity, 2018
Sylvia Plath medal for poetry creativity, 2017
Jack Kerouac poetry merit award, 2016
Arthur Rimbaud merit diploma, 2015
Nazik al Malieka literary prize, 2012
Alexandria public library prize for poetry creativity, 2012
Naji Namman international literary prize for writing poetry, 2014 Shurouk Hammoud: a Syrian poetess, journalist and litcrary translator.
She has five published poetry collections.
Award winner of many poetry awards:
Charles Baudelaire first prize for poetry creativity, 2018
Sylvia Plath medal for poetry creativity, 2017
Jack Kerouac poetry merit award, 2016
Arthur Rimbaud merit diploma, 2015
Nazik al Malieka literary prize, 2012
Alexandria public library prize for poetry creativity, 2012
Naji Namman international literary prize for writing poetry, 2014

She has been appointed as ambassador of the word by Cesar Egido Serrano foundation, 2016

Her poetry has been translated into French, Finnish, Mandarin, German, and Italian.

She has been appointed as ambassador of the word by Cesar Egido Serrano foundation, 2016

Her poetry has been translated into French, Finnish, Mandarin, German, and Italian.

My handbag

My handbag is full of caution
Buttons of all sizes
For sudden holes
Needle and black threads
To sew wounds of heart and clothing as well
Empty sanitary bags for vomiting cases that occur to those
who live here nowadays
Wet wipes to wipe make up' shredders.
My handbag is full of futility
Polisher for my shoes those expired by long roads
A mobile phone that is full of people 'names I cannot any
longer remember
My poor quality glasses
My optometrist prescribed
On the pretext that I do not see beyond my nose
Dry cigarettes and a lighter that staggers genetically
Dried flowers and poems whose papers did not
accommodate
Hankies those got tired of farewells
And you ask me why does my back hurt?

I am not here

I am not here
I am not listening to you
Some clamor had forgotten to end the call in my head
Opening my windows to the night's rusty tables,
To knives those still stuck in the necks of lovers,
Coffins the night composed on the tune of waiting,
Soldiers' shoes which lost their owners,
Bags the vacuum has burdened,
Seas which belch the prayers of the ones who died on their
way to life,
Songs those mock the departed,
A sky that tightens the dawn's ear,
Houses which changed their names,
Flags whose colors got throaty
And barricades whose sands ran away from the noise of
their voices...
To awakening speeches
But no one left to read,
So please; do not scratch my silence
I am not with you
Some tomb had forgotten the phone hanged on inside my
head
Then turned the curtain down.

Interview with the remains of a Syrian man

What did the war do with the air
-it furnished it with heartbreaks,
With canned salt and smoke.
What were you waiting for before you died?
-I was waiting for a dawn's smile I painted as a lover in my
imagination.
What the trees dream about when you told them about the
wind that would take you?
-they dreamed of dancing
They dreamed of many other things they did not say a word
about.
Was there other space that rains in your daydreams?
-yes and in my night dreams it got me; so I got pregnant
with another alienation.
Are you the same person before and after the war?
-no one comes back from war empty-handed.

Anwer Ghani

Anwer Ghani is an award winner poet from Iraq. He was born in 1973 in Babylon. His name has appeared in more than thirty literary magazines and ten anthologies in USA, UK and Asia and he has won many prizes; one of them is the "World Laureate-Best Poet in 2017 from WNWU". In 2018 he was nominated to Adelaide Award for poetry and in 2019 he is the nomanee of Rock Pebbles Literary Award. Anwer is a religious scholar and consultant nephrologist and the author of more than eighty books; thirteenth of them are in English like; "Narratolyric writing"; (2016),"Antipoetic Poems";(2017) and "Mosaicked Poems"; (2018), "The Styles of Poetry"; 2019.

Blog: anwerghani2.wordpress.com

Amazon: amazon.com/author/anwerghani

Colored Hearts

The hearts of birds are so hidden so I can't see them very well. Sometimes I decide to open my sorcerous woody box to see the exact color of these runaway hearts. They are very antique and when you want to overturn their leaves you will smell the perfumes of the old southern adventures. No moon can sit in the corners of these colored hearts because their brilliant rays will blind the daring eyes of the sun.

No clear roads in the depth, just wide space its infinite moments amaze your heart. I feel it; this amazement penetrating us as an old tale. On its hand we find all the colored souls which put on our lips eternal kisses. Their hands rain astonishment over our heads and their smiles plant the colored roses in our corners. Please touch them softly; they are as delicate as a dream of a shy girl.

When we saw these colored shadows, their whispers penetrated us very fast, and when we smell the fragrance of their revelations, the sun slept in our dreams as a blue butterfly. In a matchless moment; an absent moment, all the warm letters and the deep ecstasies dissolve in us as sugar; that is when we touched these shadows and heard their colored wishes.

Pale Land

This is what I see, what I feel and what my moments talk with. I am from here; from this earth; the title of pallor. No moon here and no lovers; nothing here just pale tears. I will go deeply in the pain's tales. I will hide from the life eyes because I am just a pale remnant.

Please touch me but touch me smoothly because I am a pale remnant. My mouth is full with absence and my heart is filled with illusion. Please touch me; I want to feel my self and to know that I am a pale soul; I mean a cheap soul. Here in my land everything is pale and liking to hide even me. Here, in my land; the land of pale tears, everything is sad and pale even the sun.

The blood colors our brooks with its redness but it lets our faces very pale. I am from the pale land where you can't see colored flowers and can't hear melodic birds. Look at our boys; they are pale and look at our girls; they are pale. The trees here are pale, the rivers are pale and the hearts are pale. Our lips are pale, our hands are pale and our eyes are pale. In fact, we are just pale remnants.

The Old Castle

We have an old castle we inherited from our ancestors. Its mantle is grey, and its rivers are very short. They had made its legs from the clipped bamboo and its head from the seething tales but when you open its bone you will find just timeworn paper, and when we try to kiss its mouth there is nothing but illusions.

Yes, I know that you have high castles I need very potent eyes to see their middle ornaments but their trees know very well that the lovely wells are thirsty and their pale leaves fall on my head with the sad stories. Yes, I know that I have a very old castle vaporizing every night with smooth winds, but my grandfather said that those wind are coming from the high castle.

Yes, our hands are so coarse, and our trees are so brown but there are nothing in our hearts but breezy tales. Our eyes can see the sunset with its amazing colors when it sleeps near our castle. You should take a step to see our magic afternoons and to hear the very melodic chants of our birds. Despite our sad rivers, we don't attempt to plant tears in your fields and despite our love for your cream

Remembering

our fallen soldiers of verse

Janet Perkins Caldwell
February 14, 1959 ~ September 20, 2016

Alan W. Jankowski
16 March 1961 ~ 10 March 2017

Inner Child Press

News

We are so excited to announce the New and upcoming books of some of our Poetry Posse authors.

On the following pages we present to you ...

Jackie Davis Allen

Gail Weston Shazor

hülya n. yılmaz

Nizar Sartawi

Faleeha Hassan

Fahredin Shehu

Caroline 'Ceri' Nazareno

Eliza Segiet

William S. Peters, Sr.

No Illusions

Through the Looking Glass

Jackie Davis Allen

Now Available at
www.innerchildpress.com

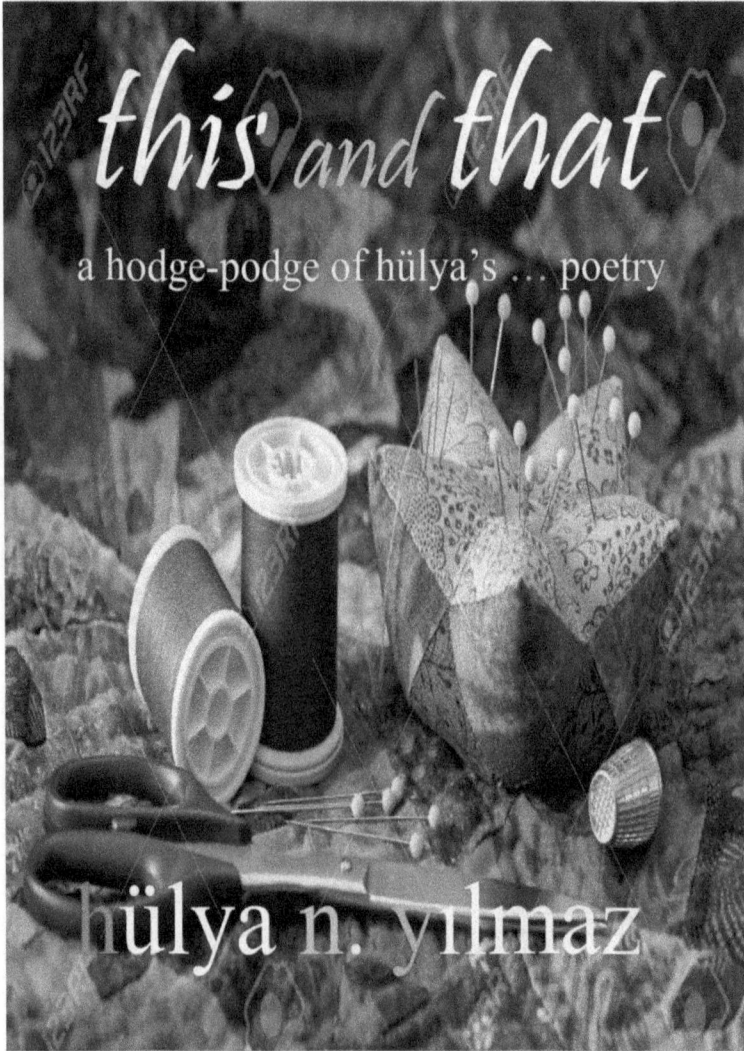

this and that

a hodge-podge of hülya's ... poetry

hülya n. yılmaz

Now Available at
www.innerchildpress.com

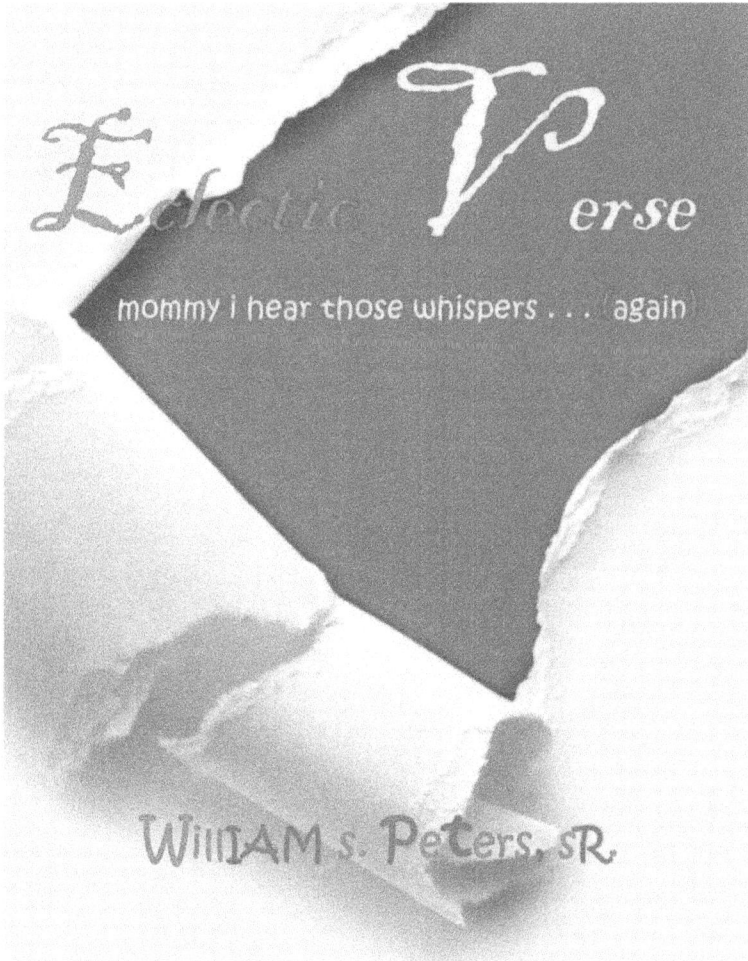

Inner Child Press News

Now Available at
www.innerchildpress.com

HERENOW

FAHREDIN SHEHU

Now Available at
www.innerchildpress.com

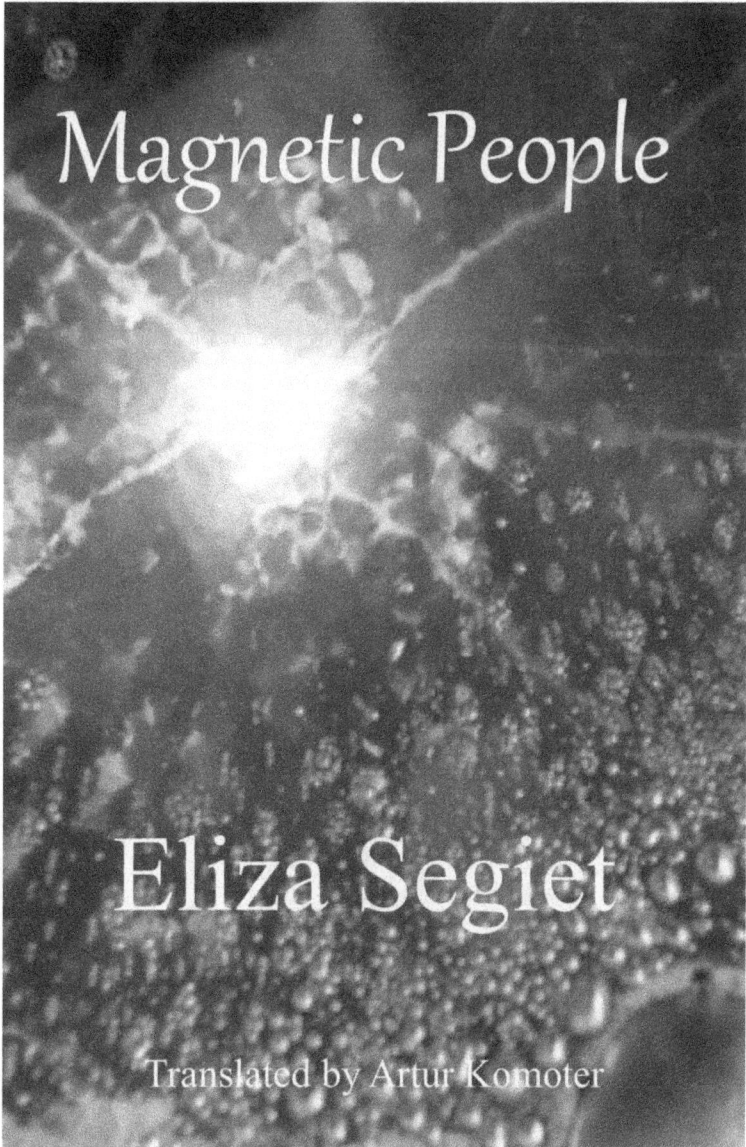

Magnetic People

Eliza Segiet

Translated by Artur Komoter

Now Available at
www.innerchildpress.com

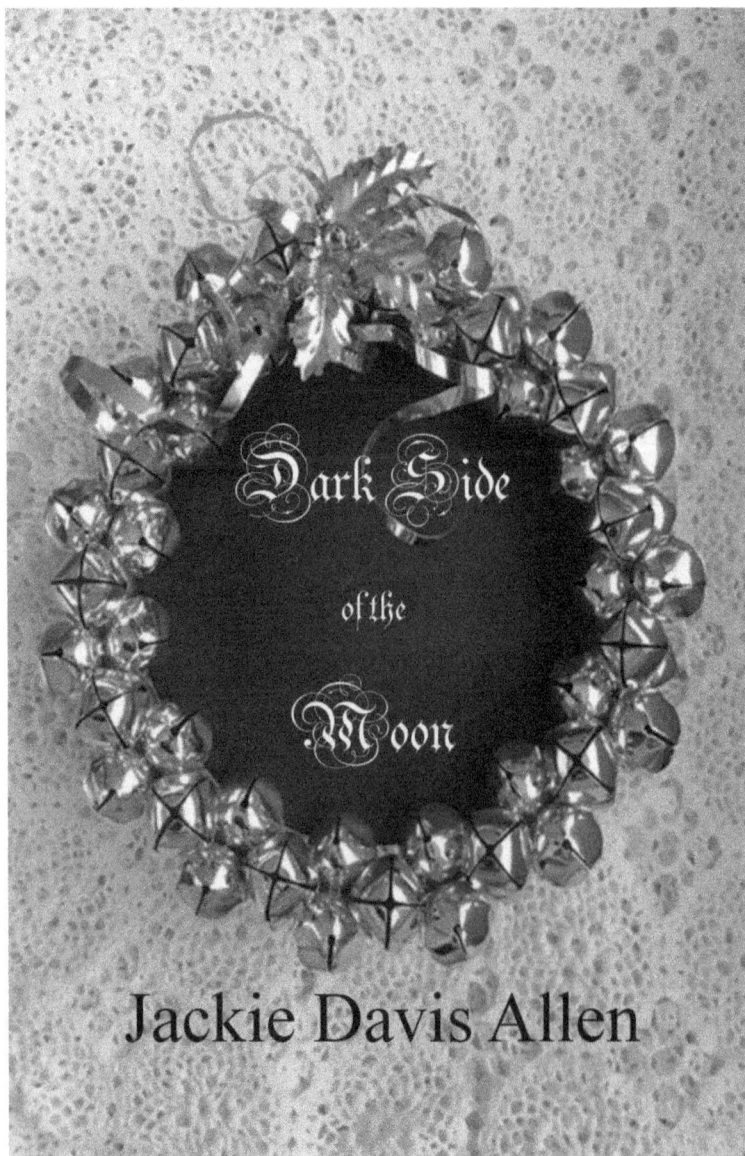

Dark Side
of the
Moon

Jackie Davis Allen

The Year of the Poet VI ~ March 2019

Now Available at
www.innerchildpress.com

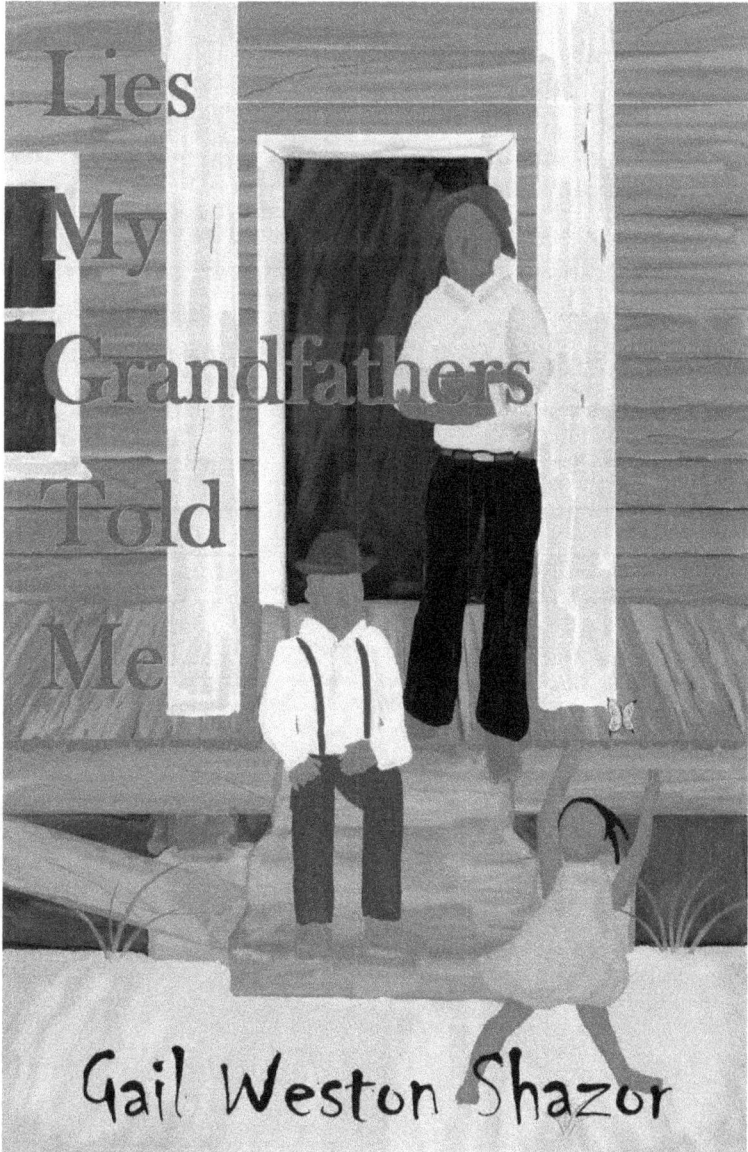

Now Available at
www.innerchildpress.com

Now Available at
www.innerchildpress.com

My Shadow

Nizar Sartawi

Mass Graves

Faleeha Hassan

Now Available at
www.innerchildpress.com

Breakfast

for

Butterflies

Faleeha Hassan

Now Available at
www.innerchildpress.com

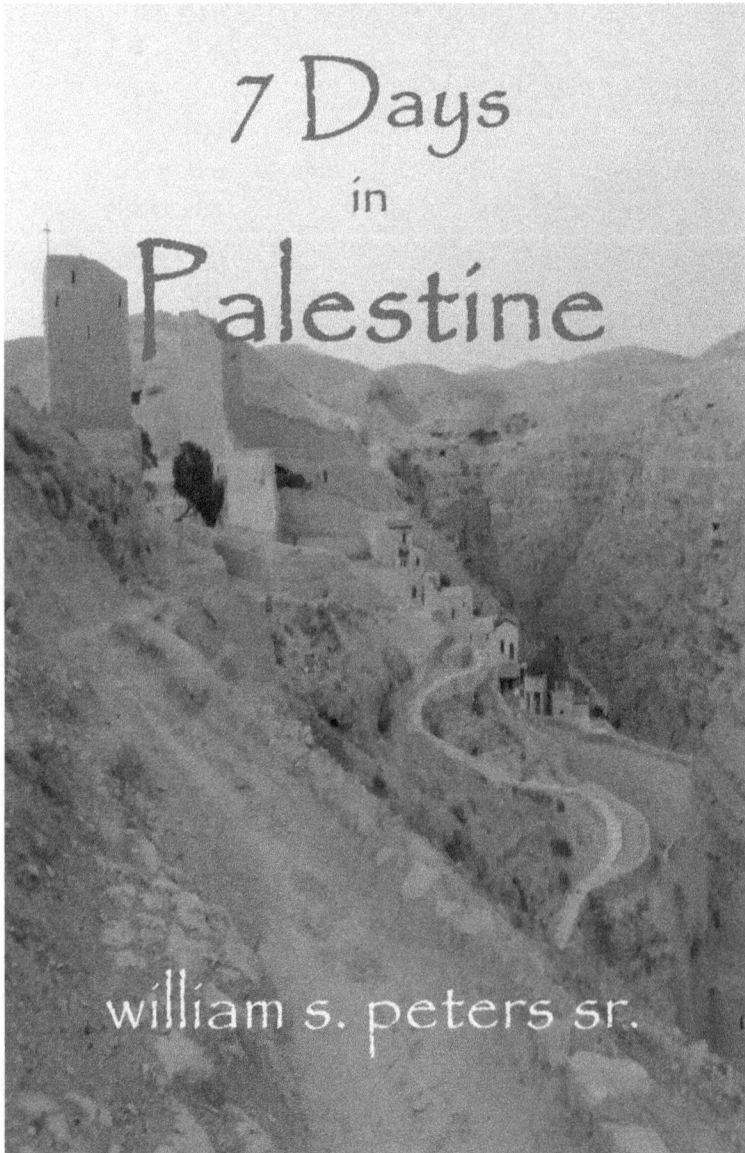

7 Days
in
Palestine

william s. peters sr.

Now Available at
www.innerchildpress.com

inner child press
presents

Tunisia My Love

william s. peters, sr.

Coming in the Summer of 2019

The Journey

Footprints and Shadows

Kosovo
Tunisia
Macedonia
Morocco
Jordan
Palestine
Israel
Italy
Turkey

a collection of poetry inspired during my travels

william s. peters, sr.

Now Available at

www.innerchildpress.com

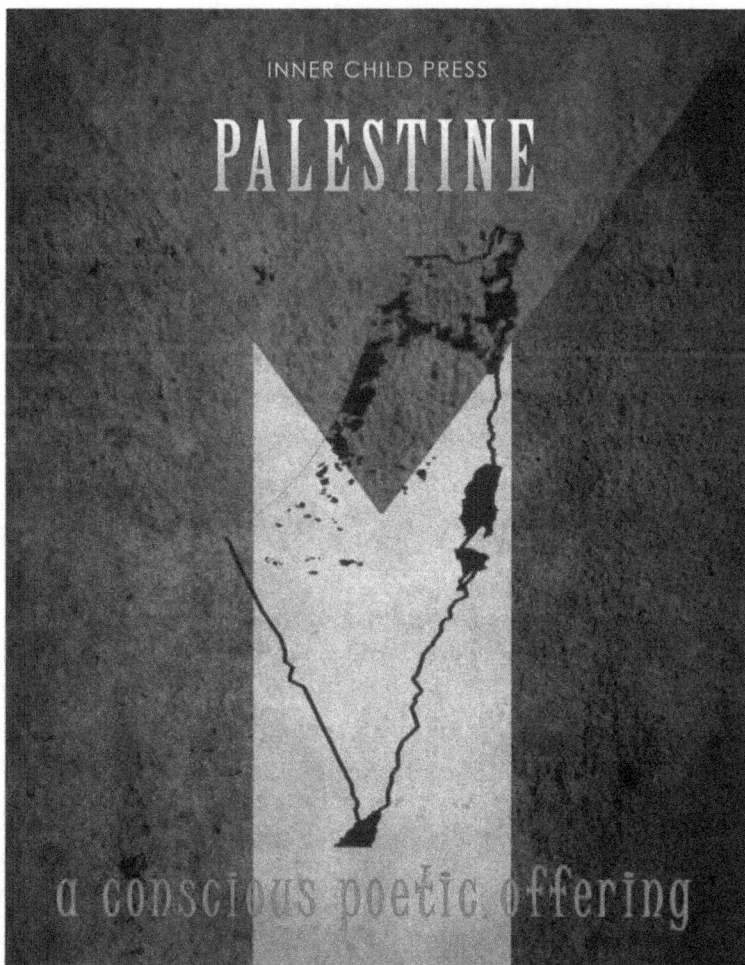

Now Available at
www.innerchildpress.com

Inner Child Press News

Now Available at
www.innerchildpress.com

Inward Reflections

Think on These Things
Book II

william s. peters, sr.

Now Available at
www.innerchildpress.com

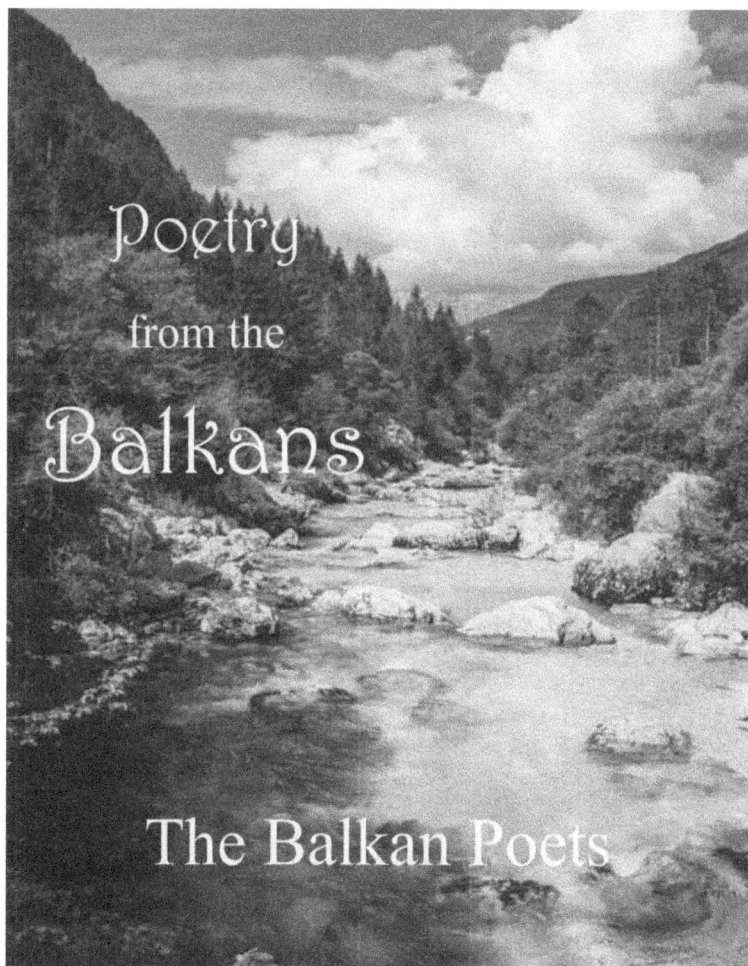

Poetry

from the

Balkans

The Balkan Poets

Other

Anthological

works from

Inner Child Press International

www.innerchildpress.com

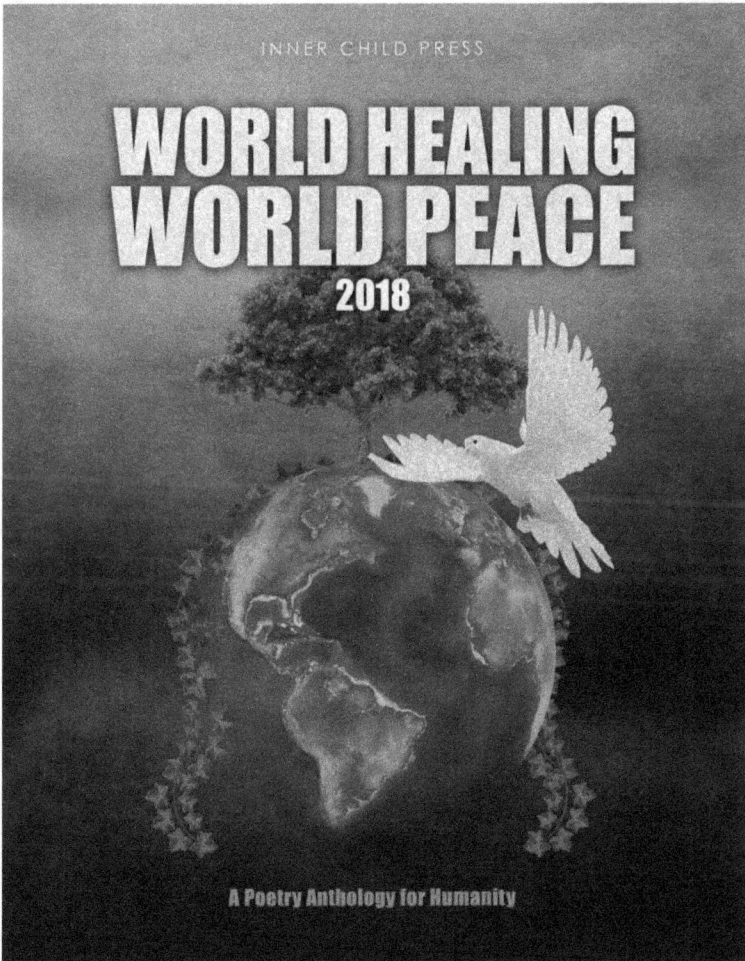

INNER CHILD PRESS

WORLD HEALING WORLD PEACE
2018

A Poetry Anthology for Humanity

Now Available

www.worldhealingworldpeacepoetry.com

Now Available

www.worldhealingworldpeacepoetry.com

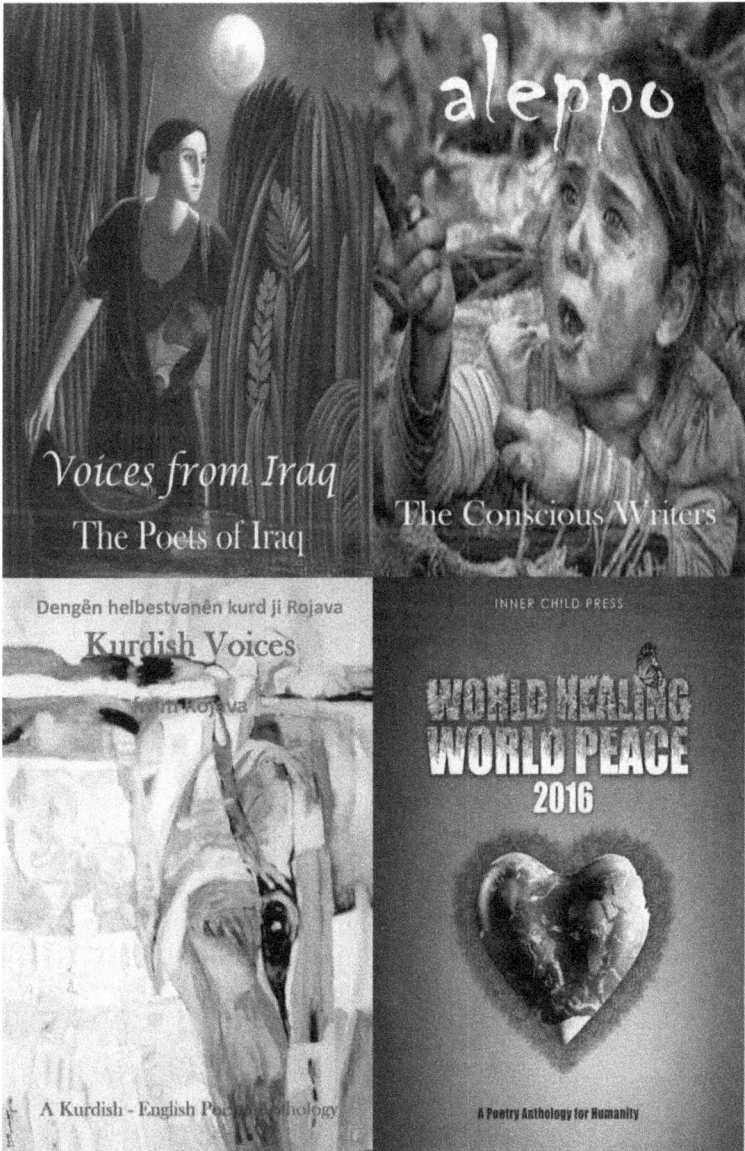

Voices from Iraq
The Poets of Iraq

aleppo
The Conscious Writers

Dengên helbestvanên kurd ji Rojava
Kurdish Voices
from Rojava
A Kurdish - English Poetry Anthology

INNER CHILD PRESS
WORLD HEALING
WORLD PEACE
2016
A Poetry Anthology for Humanity

Now Available

www.innerchildpress.com/anthologies

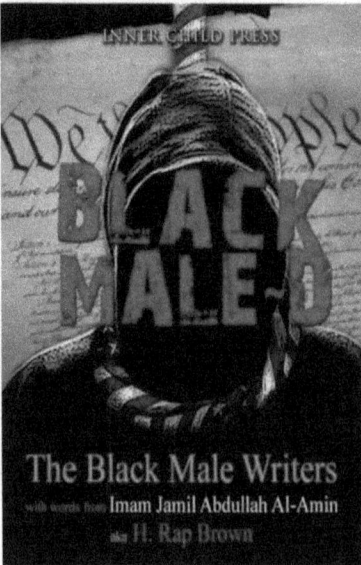

Now Available

www.innerchildpress.com/anthologies

Janet
gone too soon . . .

healing through words

Poetry ... Prose ... Prayer ... Stories

a
Poetically
Spoken
Anthology
volume I
Collector's Edition

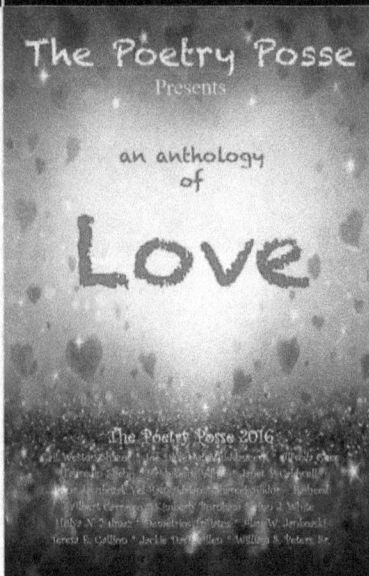

The Poetry Posse
Presents

an anthology
of

Love

The Poetry Posse 2016

Now Available

www.innerchildpress.com/anthologies

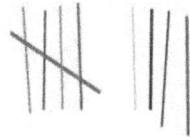

Now Available

www.innerchildpress.com/anthologies

The Year of the Poet — January 2014

The Poetry Posse

Jamie Bond
Gail Weston Shazor
Albert 'Infinite' Carrasco
Siddartha Beth Pierce
Janet P. Caldwell
June 'Bugg' Barefield
Debbie M. Allen
Tony Henninger
Joe DaVerbal Minddancer
Robert Gibbons
Neetu Wali
Shareef Abdur-Rasheed
William S. Peters, Sr.

Carnation

Our January Feature
Terri L. Johnson

the Year of the Poet — February 2014

violets

The Poetry Posse

Jamie Bond
Gail Weston Shazor
Albert 'Infinite' Carrasco
Siddartha Beth Pierce
Janet P. Caldwell
June 'Bugg' Barefield
Debbie M. Allen
Tony Henninger
Joe DaVerbal Minddancer
Robert Gibbons
Neetu Wali
Shareef Abdur-Rasheed
William S. Peters, Sr.

Our February Features
Teresa E. Gallion & Robert Gibson

the Year of the Poet — March 2014

The Poetry Posse

Jamie Bond
Gail Weston Shazor
Albert 'Infinite' Carrasco
Siddartha Beth Pierce
Janet P. Caldwell
June 'Bugg' Barefield
Debbie M. Allen
Tony Henninger
Joe DaVerbal Minddancer
Robert Gibbons
Neetu Wali
Shareef Abdur-Rasheed
Kimberly Burnham
William S. Peters, Sr.

daffodil

Our March Featured Poets
AliciaC. Cooper & hülya yılmaz

the Year of the Poet — April 2014

The Poetry Posse

Jamie Bond
Gail Weston Shazor
Albert 'Infinite' Carrasco
Siddartha Beth Pierce
Janet P. Caldwell
June 'Bugg' Barefield
Debbie M. Allen
Tony Henninger
Joe DaVerbal Minddancer
Robert Gibbons
Neetu Wali
Shareef Abdur-Rasheed
Kimberly Burnham
William S. Peters, Sr.

Sweet Pea

Our April Featured Poets
Fahredin Shehu
Martina Reisz Newberry
Justin Blackburn
Monte Smith

celebrating international poetry month

Now Available

www.innerchildpress.com/the-year-of-the-poet

172

the year of the poet
May 2014

May's Featured Poets
ReeCee
Joski the Poet
Shannon Stanton

Dedicated To our Children

The Poetry Posse

Lily of the Valley

the Year of the Poet
June 2014

Love & Relationship

Rose

June's Featured Poets
Shamelle McLin
Jacqueline D. E. Kennedy
Abraham N. Benjamin

The Poetry Posse

The Year of the Poet
July 2014

July Feature Poets
Christena A. V. Williams
Dr. John R. Strum
Kolade Olanrewaju Freedom

The Poetry Posse

Lotus
Asian Flower of the Month

The Year of the Poet
August 2014

Gladiolus

The Poetry Posse

August Feature Poets
Ann White • Rosalind Cherry • Sheila Jenkins

Now Available

The Year of the Poet
September 2014

Aster   Morning-Glory

Wild Child of September Birth Flower

September Feature Poets
Florence Malone * Keith Alan Hamilton

The Poetry Posse
Janie Bond * Gail Weston Shazor * Albert 'Infinite' Carrasco * Siddartha Beth Pierce
Janet P. Caldwell * June 'Bugg' Barefield * Debbie M. Allen * Tony Henninger
Joe DaVerbal Minddancer * Robert Gibbons * Neetu Wali * Shareef Abdur-Rasheed
Kimberly Burnham * William S. Peters, Sr.

THE YEAR OF THE POET
October 2014

Red Poppy

The Poetry Posse
Janie Bond * Gail Weston Shazor * Albert 'Infinite' Carrasco * Siddartha Beth Pierce
Janet P. Caldwell * June 'Bugg' Barefield * Debbie M. Allen * Tony Henninger
Joe DaVerbal Minddancer * Robert Gibbons * Neetu Wali * Shareef Abdur-Rasheed
Kimberly Burnham * William S. Peters, Sr.

October Feature Poets
Ceri Naz * Rajendra Padhi * Elizabeth Castillo

THE YEAR OF THE POET
November 2014

Chrysanthemum

The Poetry Posse
Janie Bond * Gail Weston Shazor * Albert 'Infinite' Carrasco * Siddartha Beth Pierce
Janet P. Caldwell * June 'Bugg' Barefield * Debbie M. Allen * Tony Henninger
Joe DaVerbal Minddancer * Robert Gibbons * Neetu Wali * Shareef Abdur-Rasheed
Kimberly Burnham * William S. Peters, Sr.

November Feature Poets
Jocelyn Mosman * Jackie Allen * James Moore * Neville Hiatt

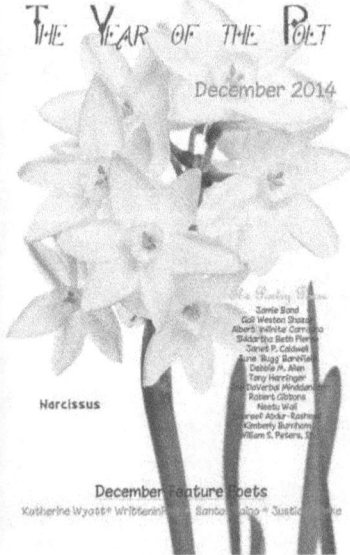

THE YEAR OF THE POET
December 2014

Narcissus

The Poetry Posse
Janie Bond
Gail Weston Shazor
Albert 'Infinite' Carrasco
Siddartha Beth Pierce
Janet P. Caldwell
June 'Bugg' Barefield
Debbie M. Allen
Tony Henninger
DaVerbal Minddancer
Robert Gibbons
Neetu Wali
Shareef Abdur-Rasheed
Kimberly Burnham
William S. Peters, Sr.

December Feature Poets
Katherine Wyatt* WritteninPrism * Santoshi Jha * Justin Pixie

Now Available

www.innerchildpress.com/the-year-of-the-poet

THE YEAR OF THE POET II
January 2015

Garnet

Jamie Bond
Gail Weston Shazor
Albert 'Infinite' Carrasco
Siddartha Beth Pierce
Janet P. Caldwell
Tony Henninger
Joe DaVerbal Minddancer
Robert Gibbons
Neetu Wali
Shareef Abdur – Rasheed
Kimberly Burnham
Ann White
Keith Alan Hamilton
Katherine Wyatt
Fahredin Shehu
Hülya N. Yılmaz
Teresa E. Gallion
Jackie Allen
William S. Peters, Sr.

January Feature Poets
Bismay Mohanti * Jen Walls * Eric Sudah

THE YEAR OF THE POET II
February 2015

Amethyst

THE POETRY POSSE
Jamie Bond
Gail Weston Shazor
Albert 'Infinite' Carrasco
Siddartha Beth Pierce
Janet P. Caldwell
Tony Henninger
Joe DaVerbal Minddancer
Robert Gibbons
Neetu Wali
Shareef Abdur – Rasheed
Kimberly Burnham
Ann White
Keith Alan Hamilton
Katherine Wyatt
Fahredin Shehu
Hülya N. Yılmaz
Teresa E. Gallion
Jackie Allen
William S. Peters, Sr.

FEBRUARY FEATURE POETS
Iram Fatima * Rob McNeil * Kerstin Centervall

The Year of the Poet II
March 2015

Our Featured Poets
Heung Sook * Anthony Arnold * Alicia Poland

Bloodstone

The Poetry Posse 2015
Jamie Bond * Gail Weston Shazor * Albert 'Infinite' Carrasco
Siddartha Beth Pierce * Janet P. Caldwell * Tony Henninger
Joe DaVerbal Minddancer * Neetu Wali * Shareef Abdur – Rasheed
Kimberly Burnham * Ann White * Keith Alan Hamilton
Katherine Wyatt * Fahredin Shehu * Hülya N. Yılmaz
Teresa E. Gallion * Jackie Allen * William S. Peters, Sr.

The Year of the Poet II
April 2015

Celebrating International Poetry Month

Our Featured Poets
Raja Williams * Dennis Ferado * Laure Charazac

Diamonds

The Poetry Posse 2015
Jamie Bond * Gail Weston Shazor * Albert 'Infinite' Carrasco
Siddartha Beth Pierce * Janet P. Caldwell * Tony Henninger
Joe DaVerbal Minddancer * Neetu Wali * Shareef Abdur – Rasheed
Kimberly Burnham * Ann White * Keith Alan Hamilton
Katherine Wyatt * Fahredin Shehu * Hülya N. Yılmaz
Teresa E. Gallion * Jackie Allen * William S. Peters, Sr.

Now Available

www.innerchildpress.com/the-year-of-the-poet

The Year of the Poet II

September 2015

Featured Poets

Alfreda Ghee   Lonneice Weeks Badley   Demetrios Trifiatis

Sapphires

The Poetry Posse 2015

Jamie Bond * Gail Weston Shazor * Albert 'Infinite' Carrasco
Siddartha Beth Pierce * Janet P. Caldwell * Tony Henninger
Joe DaVerbal Minddancer * Neetu Wali * Shareef Abdur – Rasheed
Kimberly Burnham * Ann White * Keith Alan Hamilton
Katherine Wyatt * Fahredin Shehu * Hülya N. Yılmaz
Teresa E. Gallion * Jackie Allen * William S. Peters, Sr

The Year of the Poet II

October 2015

Featured Poets

Monte Smith * Laura J. Wolfe * William Washington

Opal

The Poetry Posse 2015

Jamie Bond * Gail Weston Shazor * Albert 'Infinite' Carrasco
Siddartha Beth Pierce * Janet P. Caldwell * Tony Henninger
Joe DaVerbal Minddancer * Neetu Wali * Shareef Abdur – Rasheed
Kimberly Burnham * Ann White * Keith Alan Hamilton
Katherine Wyatt * Fahredin Shehu * Hülya N. Yılmaz
Teresa E. Gallion * Jackie Allen * William S. Peters, Sr.

The Year of the Poet II

November 2015

Featured Poets

Alan W. Jankowski
Hannie Mohanty
Janet Moore

Topaz

The Poetry Posse 2015

Jamie Bond * Gail Weston Shazor * Albert 'Infinite' Carrasco
Siddartha Beth Pierce * Janet P. Caldwell * Tony Henninger
Joe DaVerbal Minddancer * Neetu Wali * Shareef Abdur – Rasheed
Kimberly Burnham * Ann White * Keith Alan Hamilton
Katherine Wyatt * Fahredin Shehu * Hülya N. Yılmaz
Teresa E. Gallion * Jackie Allen * William S. Peters, Sr.

The Year of the Poet II

December 2015

Featured Poets

Kerione Bryan * Michelle Joan Barulich * Neville Hiatt

Turquoise

The Poetry Posse 2015

Jamie Bond * Gail Weston Shazor * Albert 'Infinite' Carrasco
Siddartha Beth Pierce * Janet P. Caldwell * Tony Henninger
Joe DaVerbal Minddancer * Neetu Wali * Shareef Abdur – Rasheed
Kimberly Burnham * Ann White * Keith Alan Hamilton
Katherine Wyatt * Fahredin Shehu * Hülya N. Yılmaz
Teresa E. Gallion * Jackie Allen * William S. Peters, Sr.

Now Available

www.innerchildpress.com/the-year-of-the-poet

The Year of the Poet III
January 2016

Featured Poets

Lana Joseph * Atom Cyrus Rush * Christona Williams

Dark-eyed Junco

The Poetry Posse 2016

Gail Weston Shazor * Shine Jakubczak-Vel Rattystabalos * Ann J. Wylie
Edwaldo Shebu * Jehbhlach Padigos * Janet P. Caldwell
Joe DaVerbal Minddancer * Shareef Abdur - Rasheed
Albert Carrasco * Kimberly Burnham * Keith Allen Hamilton
Hülya N. Yılmaz * Demetrios Trifiatis * Allen W. Jankowski
Teresa E. Gallion * Jackie Davis Allen * William S. Peters, Sr.

The Year of the Poet III
February 2016

Featured Poets

Anthony Arnold
Anna Chalasz
Andra Hawthorne

Puffin

The Poetry Posse 2016

Gail Weston Shazor * Joe DaVerbal Minddancer * Fahredin Ghee
Edwaldo Shebu * Jehbhlach Padigos * Janet P. Caldwell
Shine Jakubczak-Vel Rattystabalos * Shareef Abdur - Rasheed
Albert Carrasco * Kimberly Burnham * Ann J. Wylie
Hülya N. Yılmaz * Demetrios Trifiatis * Allen W. Jankowski
Teresa E. Gallion * Jackie Davis Allen * William S. Peters, Sr.

The Year of the Poet
March 2016
Featured Poets

Jeton Kelmendi   Nizar Sartawi   Sami Muhanna

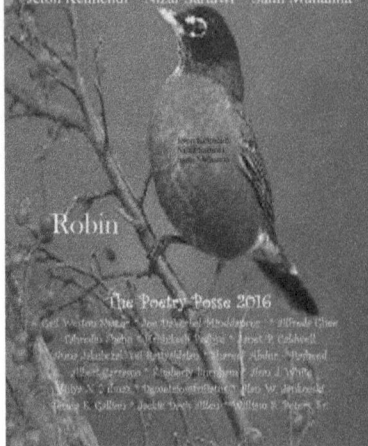

Robin

The Poetry Posse 2016

Gail Weston Shazor * Joe DaVerbal Minddancer * Alfredo Ghee
Edwaldo Shebu * Jehbhlach Padigos * Janet P. Caldwell
Shine Jakubczak-Vel Rattystabalos * Shareef Abdur - Rasheed
Albert Carrasco * Kimberly Burnham * Ann J. Wylie
Hülya N. Yılmaz * Demetrios Trifiatis * Allen W. Jankowski
Teresa E. Gallion * Jackie Davis Allen * William S. Peters, Sr.

The Year of the Poet III

Featured Poets

Ali Abdolrezaei

Anna Chalasz

Agin Vinca

Ceri Naz

Black Capped Chickadee

The Poetry Posse 2016

Gail Weston Shazor * Joe DaVerbal Minddancer * Alfredo Ghee
Fahredin Shehu * Jehbhlach Padigos * Janet P. Caldwell
Anna Jakubczak Vel Ratty Adalan * Shareef Abdur - Rasheed
Albert Carrasco * Kimberly Burnham * Ann J. Wylie
Hülya N. Yılmaz * Demetrios Trifiatis * Allen W. Jankowski
Teresa E. Gallion * Jackie Davis Allen * William S. Peters, Sr.

celebrating international poetry month

Now Available

www.innerchildpress.com/the-year-of-the-poet

The Year of the Poet
May 2016

Bob Strum
Barbara Allan
D.L. Davis

Oriole

The Year of the Poet III
June 2016

Featured Poets

Qibrije Demiri- Frangu
Naime Beqiraj
Faleeba Hassan
Bedri Zyberaj

Black Necked Stilt

The Poetry Posse 2016

The Year of the Poet III
July 2016

Featured Poets

Tram Fatima 'Ashi'
Langley Shazor
Jody Doty
Emilia T. Davis

Indigo Bunting

The Poetry Posse 2016

The Year of the Poet III
August 2016

Featured Poets

Anita Dash
Irena Jovanovic
Malgorzata Gouluda

Painted Bunting

The Poetry Posse 2016

Now Available

www.innerchildpress.com/the-year-of-the-poet

The Year of the Poet III
September 2016

Featured Poets

Simone Weber
Abhijit Sen
Eunice Barbara C. Novio

Long Billed Curle

The Poetry Posse 2016

The Year of the Poet III
October 2016

Featured Poets

Leon Joseph
Krishnamoorthy
James Moore

Barn Owl

The Poetry Posse 2016

The Year of the Poet III
November 2016

Featured Poets

Rosemary Burns
Robin Ouzman Hislop
Lonneice Weeks-Badley

Northern Cardinal

The Poetry Posse 2016

The Year of the Poet III
December 2016

Featured Poets

Samih Masoud
Mountassir Aziz Bien
Abdulkadir Musa

Rough Legged Hawk

The Poetry Posse 2016

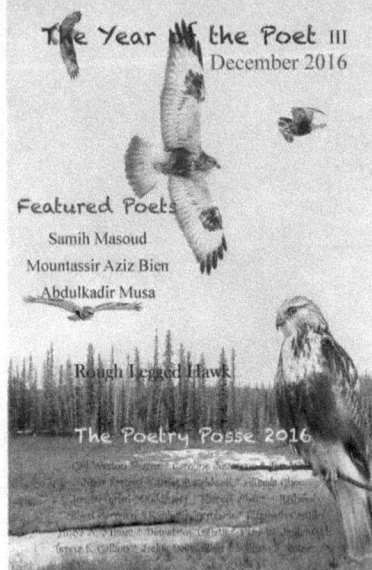

Now Available

www.innerchildpress.com/the-year-of-the-poet

The Year of the Poet IV
January 2017

Featured Poets

Jon Minell
Natalie Shields
Irani Fatima 'Ashi

Quaking Aspen

The Poetry Posse 2017

Gail Weston Shazor * Caroline Nazareno * Bunny Mohanty
Nizar Sartawi * Anna Jakubczak Vel Ratty Adalan * Jan Wells
Joe DaVerbal Minddancer * Shareef Abdur – Rasheed
Albert Carrasco * Kimberly Burnham * Elizabeth Castillo
Hülya N. Yılmaz * Teleasha Hanson * Allen W. Jankowski
Teresa E. Gallion * Jackie 'Devi' Allen * William S. Peters, Sr

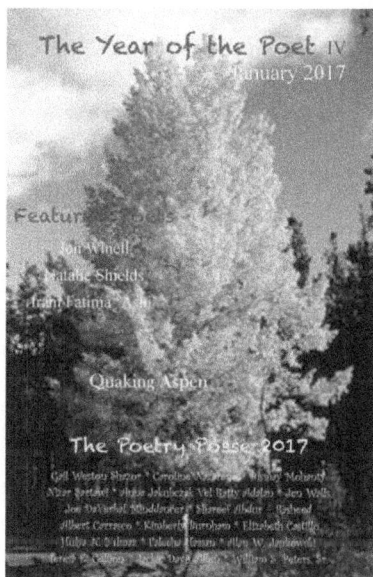

The Year of the Poet IV
February 2017

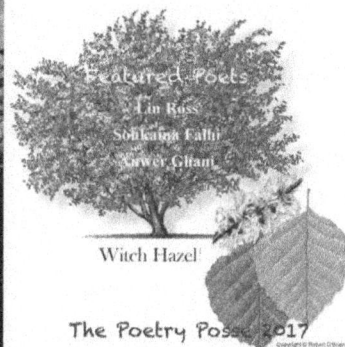

Featured Poets

Lin Ross
Sohkatya Fathi
Grwer Gitani

Witch Hazel

The Poetry Posse 2017

Gail Weston Shazor * Caroline Nazareno * Bunny Mohanty
Nizar Sartawi * Anna Jakubczak Vel Ratty Adalan * Jan Wells
Joe DaVerbal Minddancer * Shareef Abdur – Rasheed
Albert Carrasco * Kimberly Burnham * Elizabeth Castillo
Hülya N. Yılmaz * Teleasha Hanson * Allen W. Jankowski
Teresa E. Gallion * Jackie 'Devi' Allen * William S. Peters, Sr

The Year of the Poet IV
March 2017

Featured Poets

Tremell Stevens
Francisca Ricinski
Jamil Abu Shaih

The Eastern Redbud

The Poetry Posse 2017

Gail Weston Shazor * Caroline Nazareno * Bunny Mohanty
Teresa E. Gallion * Anna Jakubczak Vel Ratty Adalan
Joe DaVerbal Minddancer * Shareef Abdur – Rasheed
Albert Carrasco * Kimberly Burnham * Elizabeth Castillo
Hülya N. Yılmaz * Teleasha Hanson * Jackie 'Devi' Allen
Jan Wells * Nizar Sartawi * * William S. Peters, Sr

The Year of the Poet IV
April 2017

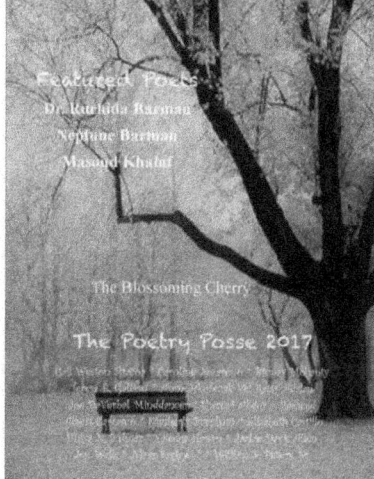

Featured Poets

Dr. Rachida Barman
Neptune Barman
Masund Khabif

The Blossoming Cherry

The Poetry Posse 2017

Now Available

The Year of the Poet IV
May 2017

The Flowering Dogwood Tree

Featured Poets
Kallisa Powell
Alicja Maria Kuberska
Fethi Sassi

The Poetry Posse 2017

Gail Weston Shazor * Caroline Nazareno * Tzemin Mohanty
Teresa E. Gallion * Anna Jakubczak Vel Ratty Adalan
Joe DaVerbal Minddancer * Shareef Abdur – Rasheed
Albert Carrasco * Kimberly Burnham * Elizabeth Castillo
Hülya N. Yılmaz * Faleeha Hassan * Jackie Davis Allen
Jen Walls * Nizar Sartawi * * William S. Peters, Sr.

The Year of the Poet IV
June 2017

Featured Poets
Eliza Segiet
Tze-Min Tsai
Abdulla Issa

The Linden Tree

The Poetry Posse 2017

Hülya N. Yılmaz * Jen Walls * Nizar Sartawi * William S. Peters, Sr.

The Year of the Poet IV
July 2017

Featured Poets
Anca Mihaela Bruma
Ibaa Ismail
Zvonko Taneski

The Oak Moon

The Poetry Posse 2017

The Year of the Poet IV
August 2017

Featured Poets
Jonathan Aquino
Kitty Hsu
Langley Shazor

The Hazelnut Tree

The Poetry Posse 2017

Gail Weston Shazor * Caroline Nazareno *
Teresa E. Gallion * Anna Jakubczak Vel Ratty Adalan
Joe DaVerbal Minddancer * Shareef Abdur – Rasheed
Albert Carrasco * Kimberly Burnham * Elizabeth Castillo
Hülya N. Yılmaz * Faleeha Hassan * Jackie Davis Allen
Jen Walls * Nizar Sartawi * * William S. Peters, Sr.

Now Available

www.innerchildpress.com/the-year-of-the-poet

The Year of the Poet IV
September 2017

Featured Poets

Martina Reisz Newber
Ameer Nassir
Christine Fulco Nea
Robert Neal

The Elm Tree

The Poetry Posse 2017

Gail Weston Shazor * Caroline Nazareno * Bismay Mohanty
Teresa E. Gallion * Anna Jakubczak Vel Ratty Adalan
Joe DaVerbal Minddancer * Shareef Abdur – Rasheed
Albert Carrasco * Kimberly Burnham * Elizabeth Castillo
Hülya N. Yılmaz * Faleeha Hassan * Jackie Davis Allen
Jen Walls * Nizar Sartawi * * William S. Peters, Sr.

The Year of the Poet IV
October 2017

Featured Poets

Ahmed Abu Saleem
Nedal Al-Qaeim
Sadeddin Shahin

The Black Walnut Tree

The Poetry Posse 2017

Gail Weston Shazor * Caroline Nazareno * Bismay Mohanty
Teresa E. Gallion * Anna Jakubczak Vel Ratty Adalan
Joe DaVerbal Minddancer * Shareef Abdur – Rasheed
Albert Carrasco * Kimberly Burnham * Elizabeth Castillo
Hülya N. Yılmaz * Faleeha Hassan * Jackie Davis Allen
Jen Walls * Nizar Sartawi * * William S. Peters, Sr.

The Year of the Poet IV
November 2017

Featured Poets

Kay Peters
Alfreda D. Ghee
Gabriella Garofalo
Rosemary Cappello

The Tree of Life

The Poetry Posse 2017

Gail Weston Shazor * Caroline Nazareno * Bismay Mohanty
Teresa E. Gallion * Anna Jakubczak Vel Ratty Adalan
Joe DaVerbal Minddancer * Shareef Abdur – Rasheed
Albert Carrasco * Kimberly Burnham * Elizabeth Castillo
Hülya N. Yılmaz * Faleeha Hassan * Jackie Davis Allen
Jen Walls * Nizar Sartawi * William S. Peters, Sr.

The Year of the Poet IV
December 2017

Featured Poets

Justice Clarke
Mariel M. Pabroa
Kiley Brown

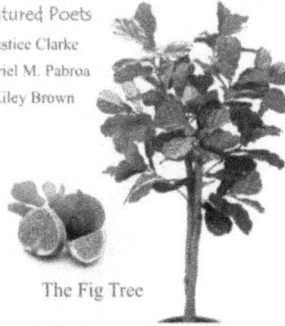

The Fig Tree

The Poetry Posse 2017

Gail Weston Shazor * Caroline Nazareno * Bismay Mohanty
Teresa E. Gallion * Anna Jakubczak Vel Ratty Adalan
Joe DaVerbal Minddancer * Shareef Abdur – Rasheed
Albert Carrasco * Kimberly Burnham * Elizabeth Castillo
Hülya N. Yılmaz * Faleeha Hassan * Jackie Davis Allen
Jen Walls * Nizar Sartawi * William S. Peters, Sr.

Now Available

www.innerchildpress.com/the-year-of-the-poet

The Year of the Poet V
January 2018

Featured Poets

Iyad Shamasnah

Yasmeen Hamzeh

Ali Abdolrezaei

Aksum

The Poetry Posse 2018

Gail Weston Shazor * Caroline Nazareno * Tezmin Ition Tsai
Hülya N. Yılmaz * Faleeha Hassan * Jackie Davis Allen
Teresa E. Gallion * Anna Jakubczak Vel Ratty Adalan
Alicja Maria Kuberska * Shareef Abdur – Rasheed
Kimberly Burnham * Elizabeth Castillo
Nizar Sartawi * William S. Peters, Sr.

The Year of the Poet V
February 2018

Sabean

Featured Poets

Muhammad Azram

Anna Szawracka

Abhilipsa Kuanar

Aanika Aery

The Poetry Posse 2018

Gail Weston Shazor * Caroline Nazareno * Tezmin Ition Tsai
Hülya N. Yılmaz * Faleeha Hassan * Jackie Davis Allen
Teresa E. Gallion * Anna Jakubczak Vel Ratty Adalan
Alicja Maria Kuberska * Shareef Abdur – Rasheed
Kimberly Burnham * Elizabeth Castillo
Nizar Sartawi * William S. Peters, Sr.

The Year of the Poet V
March 2018

Featured Poets

Iram Fatima 'Aabi'
Cassandra Swan
Jaleel Khazwal
Shazia Zaman

Mexico   Cuba

Caribbean
&
Middle America

The Poetry Posse 2018

Gail Weston Shazor * Nizar Sartawi * Hülya N. Yılmaz
Jackie Davis Allen * Caroline 'Ceri' Nazareno
Alicja Maria Kuberska * Teresa E. Gallion
Faleeha Hassan * Shareef Abdur – Rasheed
Kimberly Burnham * Elizabeth Castillo
Tezmin Ition Tsai * William S. Peters, Sr.

The Year of the Poet V
April 2018

Featured Poets

The Nez Perce

The Poetry Posse 2018

Now Available

www.innerchildpress.com/the-year-of-the-poet

The Year of the Poet V

May 2018

Featured Poets

The Sumerians

The Poetry Posse 2018

Gail Weston Shazor * Nizar Sartawi * Hülya N. Yılmaz
Jackie Davis Allen * Caroline 'Ceri' Nazareno
Alicja Maria Kuberska * Teresa E. Gallion
Kimberly Burnham * Shareef Abdur – Rasheed
Faleeha Hassan * Elizabeth Castillo * Swapna Behera
Tezmin Ition Tsai * William S. Peters, Sr.

The Year of the Poet V

June 2018

Featured Poets

Bilall Maliqi * Daim Miftari * Gojko Božović * Sofija Zivković

The Paleo Indians

The Poetry Posse 2018

The Year of the Poet V

July 2018

Oceania

The Poetry Posse 2018

The Year of the Poet V

August 2018

Featured Poets

Hussein Habasch * Mircea Dan Duta * Naida Mujkić * Swagat Das

The Lapita

The Poetry Posse 2018

Gail Weston Shazor * Nizar Sartawi * Hülya N. Yılmaz
Jackie Davis Allen * Caroline 'Ceri' Nazareno
Alicja Maria Kuberska * Teresa E. Gallion
Kimberly Burnham * Shareef Abdur – Rasheed
Ashok K. Bhargava * Elizabeth Castillo * Swapna Behera
Tezmin Ition Tsai * William S. Peters, Sr.

Now Available

www.innerchildpress.com/the-year-of-the-poet

The Year of the Poet V
September 2018

The Aztecs & Incas

Featured Poets
Kolade Olanrewaju Freedom
Eliza Segiet
Mazher Hussain Abdul Ghani
Lily Swarn

The Poetry Posse 2018

Gail Weston Shazor * Nizar Sartawi * Hülya N. Yılmaz
Jackie Davis Allen * Caroline 'Ceri' Nazareno
Alicja Maria Kuberska * Teresa E. Gallion
Kimberly Burnham * Shareef Abdur – Rasheed
Ashok K. Bhargava * Elizabeth Castillo * Swapna Behera
Tezmin Ition Tsai * William S. Peters. Sr.

The Year of the Poet V
October 2018

Featured Poets
Alicia Minjarez * Lonneice Weeks-Badley
Eopamudra Mishra * Abdelwahed Souayah

Bengali

The Poetry Posse 2018

Gail Weston Shazor * Nizar Sartawi * Hülya N. Yılmaz
Jackie Davis Allen * Caroline 'Ceri' Nazareno
Alicja Maria Kuberska * Teresa E. Gallion
Kimberly Burnham * Shareef Abdur – Rasheed
Ashok K. Bhargava * Elizabeth Castillo * Swapna Behera
Tezmin Ition Tsai * William S. Peters. Sr.

The Year of the Poet V
November 2018

Featured Poets
Michelle Joan Barulich * Monsif Beroual
Krystyna Konecka * Nassira Nezzar

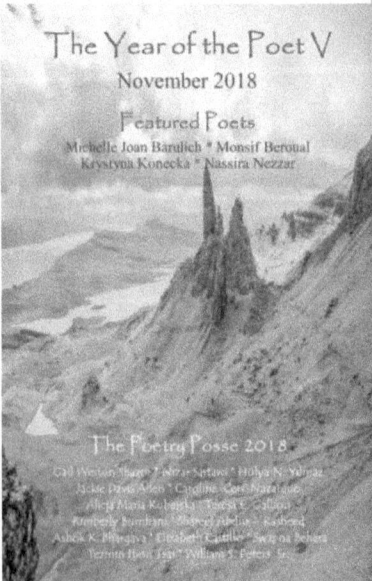

The Poetry Posse 2018

Gail Weston Shazor * Nizar Sartawi * Hülya N. Yılmaz
Jackie Davis Allen * Caroline 'Ceri' Nazareno
Alicja Maria Kuberska * Teresa E. Gallion
Kimberly Burnham * Shareef Abdur – Rasheed
Ashok K. Bhargava * Elizabeth Castillo * Swapna Behera
Tezmin Ition Tsai * William S. Peters. Sr.

The Year of the Poet V
December 2018

Featured Poets
Rose Terranova Cirigliano
Joanna Kalinowska
Sokolović Emir
Dr. T. Ashok Chakravarthy

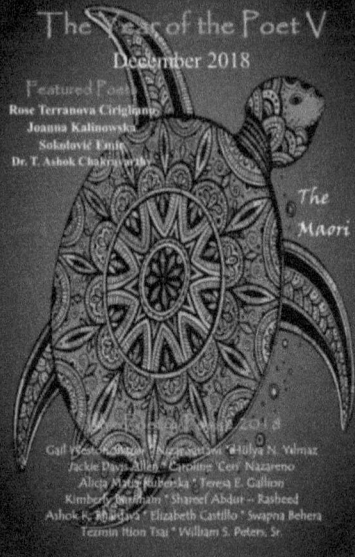

The Maori

The Poetry Posse 2018

Gail Weston Shazor * Nizar Sartawi * Hülya N. Yılmaz
Jackie Davis Allen * Caroline 'Ceri' Nazareno
Alicja Maria Kuberska * Teresa E. Gallion
Kimberly Burnham * Shareef Abdur – Rasheed
Ashok K. Bhargava * Elizabeth Castillo * Swapna Behera
Tezmin Ition Tsai * William S. Peters. Sr.

Now Available

www.innerchildpress.com/the-year-of-the-poet

The Year of the Poet VI
January 2019

Indigenous North Americans

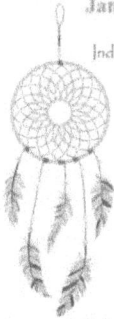

Featured Poets

Hyuda Elfehtali
Anthony Briscoe
Iram Fatima 'Ashi'
Dr. K. K. Mathew

Dream Catcher
The Poetry Posse 2019

Gail Weston Shazor * Joe Paire * Hülya N. Yılmaz
Jackie Davis Allen * Caroline 'Ceri' Naziruddin
Aluja Maria Kubenska * Teresa E. Gallion
Kimberly Burnham * Shareef Abdur + Rasheed
Ashok K. Bhargava * Elizabeth Castillo * Swapna Behera
Yasmin Riom Tsai * William S. Peters, Sr

The Year of the Poet VI
February 2019

Featured Poets
Marek Lukaszewicz * Bharati Nayak
Aida G. Roque * Jean-Jacques Fournier

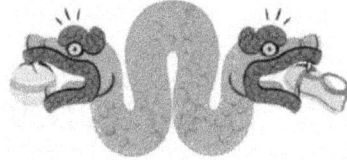

Meso-America
The Poetry Posse 2019

Gail Weston Shazor * Albert Carassco * Hülya N. Yılmaz
Jackie Davis Allen * Caroline Nazireno * Eliza Segiet
Aluja Maria Kubenska * Teresa E. Gallion * Joe Paire
Kimberly Burnham * Shareef Abdur - Rasheed
Ashok K. Bhargava * Elizabeth Castillo * Swapna Behera
Yasmin Riom Tsai * William S. Peters, Sr

Now Available

www.innerchildpress.com/the-year-of-the-poet

and there is much, much more !

visit . . .

www.innerchildpress.com/antho
logies-sales-special.php

Also check out our Authors and
all the wonderful Books
Available at :

www.innerchildpress.com/autho
rs-pages

INNER CHILD PRESS

WORLD HEALING
WORLD PEACE
2018

A Poetry Anthology for Humanity

Now Available

www.worldhealingworldpeacepoetry.com

Now Available

www.worldhealingworldpeacepoetry.com

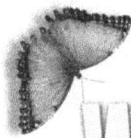

in support

World Healing
World Peace

www.worldhealingworldpeacepoetry.com

191

World Healing
World Peace
2018

Now Available

www.worldhealingworldpeacepoetry.com

Inner Child Press International

'building bridges of cultural understanding'

Meet our Cultural Ambassadors

Fahredin Shehu
Director of Cultural

Faleha Hassan
Iraq – USA

Elizabeth E. Castillo
Philippines

Antoinette Coleman
Chicago
Midwest USA

Ananda Nepali
Nepal – Bhutan
Northern India

Kimberly Burnham
Pacific Northwest
USA

Alicja Kuberska
Poland
Eastern Europe

Swapna Behera
India
Southeast Asia

Kolade O. Freedom
Nigeria
West Africa

Monsif Beroual
Morocco
Northern Africa

Ashok K. Bhargava
Canada

Tzemin Ition Tsai
Republic of China
Greater China

Alicia M. Ramírez
Mexico
Central America

Christena AV Williams
Jamaica
Caribbean

Louise Hudon
Eastern Canada

Aziz Mountassir
Morocco
Eastern Africa

Shareef Abdur-Rasheed
Southeastern USA

Laure Charazac
France
Western Europe

Mohammad Ikbal Harh
Lebanon
Middle East

Mohamed Abdel
Aziz Shmeis
Egypt
Middle East

Bilary Mainga
Malawi
Eastern Africa

Josephus R. Johnson
Liberia

www.innerchildpress.com

This Anthological Publication
is underwritten solely by

Inner Child Press

Inner Child Press is a Publishing Company
Founded and Operated by Writers. Our personal
publishing experiences provides us an intimate
understanding of the sometimes daunting
challenges Writers, New and Seasoned may face in
the Business of Publishing and Marketing their
Creative "Written Work".

For more Information

Inner Child Press

www.innerchildpress.com

Inner Child Press International

'building bridges of cultural understanding'

202 Wiltree Court, State College, Pennsylvania 16801

www.innerchildpress.com

~ fini ~

www.ingramcontent.com/pod-product-compliance
Lightning Source LLC
LaVergne TN
LVHW011154080426
835508LV00007B/399